RIFLESHOOTER
MAGAZINE'S GUIDE TO
BIG GAME HUNTING

RIFLESHOOTER
MAGAZINE'S GUIDE TO
BIG GAME HUNTING

EDITORS OF RIFLESHOOTER MAGAZINE
INTRODUCTION BY J. SCOTT RUPP

Skyhorse Publishing

Skyhorse Publishing books may be purchased in bulk at special discounts for sales promotion, corporate gifts, fund-raising, or educational purposes. Special editions can also be created to specifications. For details, contact the Special Sales Department, Skyhorse Publishing, 307 West 36th Street, 11th Floor, New York, NY 10018 or info@skyhorsepublishing.com.

Skyhorse® and Skyhorse Publishing® are registered trademarks of Skyhorse Publishing, Inc.®, a Delaware corporation.

Visit our website at www.skyhorsepublishing.com.

10 9 8 7 6 5 4 3 2 1

Library of Congress Cataloging-in-Publication Data is available on file.

Cover design by Tom Lau
Cover photo credit: J. Scott Rupp

Print ISBN: 978-1-5107-2076-3
Ebook ISBN: 978-1-5107-2079-4

Printed in China

TABLE OF CONTENTS

PART III: RIFLE KNOW-HOW

INTRODUCTION

Big game hunting is a fascinating mix of fieldcraft, marksmanship, and equipment. I'm tempted to say fieldcraft—the hunting skills that allow you to find game and get close enough to make a sure shot—is most important, but looking back on my own experiences I realize this is not always the case. Say you're hunting with a guide, for instance, or you're restricted to a particular tree stand or box blind. Here you don't have to figure out game locations, movement patterns, and the like because it's already been done for you.

In these cases, if you define the hunt as a "success" as one that ends with the harvest of an animal (and that's debatable), it's up to you and your gear. And even here it's hard to say which can have the most impact on a hunt. You can carry the latest and greatest rifle, cartridge, and optic, but if you're unable to hit anything with them, it's all moot.

Conversely, if you've picked the wrong gear, you're not exactly in high cotton. To use a couple of outlandish examples, you'd be poorly served taking a .223 with full-metal-jacket bullets for elk or a .243 with any bullet for brown bear. And it is this equipment selection, particularly cartridge and bullet choices, that dominate the thoughts of not just newcomers to hunting but also those who've been chasing big game for a long time. Certainly, these are the questions we receive most at *RifleShooter* magazine and the majority of questions I field from people I meet, particularly new folks.

And veteran hunters know these are the most entertaining discussions you can have. Laugh all you want about the age-old "Which is better, the .30-06 or the .270?" debate; there are a still lot of people out there who are willing to throw down on this argument—with feeling.

This book isn't going to definitively settle any of these debates, but it is going to give hunters of all experience levels a lot of great information about cartridges, ammunition, rifles, optics, and more. Whether your pursuits focus on North America's primary species—whitetails, mulies, elk, pronghorn, wild boar, and the like—or your tastes run to more exotic, worldwide quarry, this book has you covered. And we haven't neglected shooting skills either, as chapters on long- and close-range shooting will help you increase your competency (and, hopefully, confidence) so you can make that shot when the time comes.

J. Scott Rupp
Editor in Chief, *RifleShooter*

PART I
CALIBER PROFILES

6.5 STARTER KIT

By Layne Simpson

Thinking of trying the 6.5 for hunting? There are a lot more choices out there than you might think.

all me silly if you will, but I feel insulted when a magazine publishes a photograph of someone pointing a firearm directly at me. However, I can recall many years ago when just such a photo was one of my favorites. Only the muzzle and front sight of the rifle were in focus, and the caption at the bottom of the photo said it all: "The new .264 Winchester Magnum—it makes a helluva noise and packs a helluva punch" (or something like that).

And it did just that in the hands of hunters all across America until the 7mm Remington Magnum came along four years later.

The .264 Winchester Magnum was the second American-designed cartridge of its caliber to come along. Back in 1917, rifle designer and manufacturer Charles Newton introduced his .256 Newton, which was the hunter's .270 Winchester about a decade before that cartridge came along. On the slightly shortened .30-06 Springfield case, it was initially loaded with a 123-grain bullet at 3,100 fps and, later, a 140-grain bullet at 2,900 fps. Despite the fact that the Western Cartridge Company loaded the ammunition, the .256 Newton enjoyed but a short life.

Like Charlie Newton's fine little cartridge before it, the .264 Winchester Magnum enjoyed only a few brief moments of glory among American hunters. Designed to deliver its best performance in a 26-inch barrel, hunters kept demanding a shorter tube. They eventually got what they asked for in the Model 70 Featherweight with a 22-inch barrel, and they also got a terrible increase in muzzle blast and just .270 Winchester performance.

Other cartridges of the same caliber have fared better in other countries. The 6.5 Swedish, for example, was once the apple of every Scandinavian hunter's eye, and while quite a few still use it, each time I hunt there I see far more people using rifles in .30-06 and .308 Winchester. My guess is the 6.5 Swede has also long been the most popular cartridge of its caliber among American hunters, due mainly to the importation of thousands upon thousands of military-surplus rifles of excellent quality at bargain basement prices.

Even though I did not until recently become a fan of 6.5mm cartridges, I have owned a number of rifles chambered for them through the years. And I have used some of them to take a few head of game.

The first one, purchased while I was still in high school, was a Japanese Arisaka in 6.5x50. It was fairly accurate with Norma ammo, but I hated its awkward safety and horse-traded it away.

In those days, my high school chums and I were really into military surplus rifles, and our addiction was made possible by the fact that many were only slightly more expensive than dirt. But not all were, and the one we lusted over most but could never afford to buy was the handsome little Swedish Model 94 carbine in 6.5x55. With its 17½-inch barrel and Mannlicher-style stock it ranked just above Marilyn Monroe in desirability, but none of us ever got one.

My next 6.5, purchased many years later, was a Model 1909 Mannlicher-Schoenauer carbine, one of the most handsome firearms ever built. I still own that one, and through the years its slowpoke 160-grain bullet has accounted for a dozen or so hogs and a couple of whitetails.

Then came a pair of Winchester Model 70 Westerners in .264 Magnum, and how I wish I had kept one of them. There were also a Remington Model 600, a Remington Model 700 and a Ruger Model 77, all in 6.5 Remington Magnum. For a while, Ruger chambered its No. 1 rifle for the

6.5 Remington Magnum, and I still own one of those.

I have taken elk, pronghorn, black bear and deer with the .264 Winchester Magnum but have bumped off only a couple of deer with the 6.5 Remington Magnum. Despite the considerable difference in the sizes of their cases and the amount of powder they burn, I find the .264 Winchester Magnum to be only about 100 to 150 fps faster when both are fired in barrels of the same length.

Then there was a Krico rifle in 6.5x57 Mauser, but I never took any game with it. I have killed several deer with the 6.5 Swede, but I have taken more game with the 6.5-284 and 6.5 STW than with any other cartridge of the caliber.

I have never headed to the woods with a rifle in .260 Remington—not because I dislike it but because the only rifles I have tried it in that delivered satisfactory accuracy were heavy-barrel target jobs. I have taken only one deer with the 6.5-06, and the 6.5 Creedmoor is so new I've had the chance to kill only a pronghorn with it—out of a Ruger 77 Hawkeye with a 26-inch barrel.

Until the introduction of the 7mm Remington Magnum in 1962, metric cartridges had been ignored to death by American sportsmen, and the 6.5 suffered even more because it never had a champion among gun writers like the .270 Winchester (Jack

HANDLOAD CHART
SELECTED LOADS FOR 6.5MM CARTRIDGES

Cartridge/Bullet	Bullet Weight (gr.)	Powder Type	Powder Charge (gr.)	Muzzle Velocity (fps)
6.5x54 Mannlicher-Schoenauer, 17½-in. barrel				
Hornady RN	160	IMR 4350	39.0	2,155
.260 Remington, 22-in. barrel				
Hornady SST	129	RL-19	48.0	2,888
6.5x55 Swedish, 24-in. barrel				
Swift Scirocco	130	A-3100	49.0	2,872
6.5 Creedmoor, 26-in. barrel				
Hornady SST	129	H4350	44.0	2,922
6.5x57 Mauser, 24-in. barrel				
Hornady SST	129	IMR 4831	48.0	2,861
6.5x52 American, 22-in. barrel				
Hornady SST	129	RL-22	51.0	3,010
6.5-06, 24-in. barrel				
Nosler AccuBond	130	RL-22	54.0	3,119
6.5-284 Norma, 26-in. barrel				
Swift Scirocco	130	H50BMG	88.0	3,461
Hornady SST	129	IMR 7828	64.0	3,228
6.5 STW, 26-in. barrel				
Swift Scirocco	130	H50BMG	88.0	3,461

Notes: These maximum powder charges should be reduced by 10 percent for starting loads. All cases are Remington except RWS for the 6.5x54mm and Hornady for the 6.5-284 Norma and 6.5 Creedmoor. Federal 210 primers used in all except Federal 215 in .264 Magnum and 6.5 STW.

From left: .256 Newton, 6.5-06, 6.5x54 Mannlicher-Schoenauer, 6.5x57 Mauser, 6.5x55 Swedish, 6.5 Creedmoor, .260 Remington, 6.5x52 American, 6.5-.284 Norma, 6.5 Rem. Mag., .264 Win. Mag., 6.5 STW.

O'Connor) and .30-06 (Townsend Whelen and others) did.

When a 6.5mm cartridge was given a bit of ink, it often lost out in an apples-to-oranges comparison. O'Connor used to criticize other writers for comparing the velocities of the .270 and .30-06 when both were loaded with 150-grain bullets, saying that the comparison should be between the 130-grain .270 caliber and the 165-grain .30 caliber because they have similar sectional densities. But then he'd do the exact same thing by comparing velocities of the .270 with a 130-grain bullet to the .264 Winchester Magnum with a 140-grain bullet.

Something else that continues to hurt the 6.5s is the American hunter's preference for heavy-for-caliber bullets on the larger game while at the same time insisting that velocities be quite high.

To many hunters, any bullet under 140 grains is too light for elk, but a bullet of that weight is too heavy for cartridges up to the .264 Winchester Magnum if velocity greatly exceeding 3,000 fps is also a requirement. This is due to the fact that the extremely long bearing surface of that bullet prevents it from being driven as fast as a bullet of the same weight in a larger caliber.

Its sectional density is about the same as a .30 caliber bullet weighing 190 grains and a .338 caliber bullet weighing 240 grains. A 6.5mm bullet weighing 130 grains has about the same sectional density as a 180-grain bullet of .30 caliber and, all other things being equal, its penetration on game will be the same.

When developing the .264 Winchester Magnum, Winchester got around the problem by making only the rear section of the shank of the 140-grain Power-Point bullet groove diameter (.264 inch) and reducing the front section of the shank to bore diameter (.256 inch). That allowed a velocity of 3,200 fps in a 26-inch barrel at acceptable chamber pressures. Unfortunately, both Winchester and Remington eventually stopped loading two-diameter bullets in the .264 Winchester Magnum, resulting in about a 200 fps decrease in the velocity of factory ammo.

During the 1960s, my old friend Les Bowman, who had a great deal of hunting experience with the .264 Winchester Magnum and 6.5 Remington Magnum was convinced the best bullet for deer and elk was the Nosler 125-grain Partition. Today's under-140 choices include the 120-grain Swift A-Frame and the Barnes TSX. Those are great bullets, but I prefer the Hornady 129-grain SST and two 130-grainers: Swift Scirocco and Nosler AccuBond.

A grand classic, this Model 1909 Mannlicher-Schoenauer in 6.5x54 typifies the Old World 6.5s.

The SST is softer, making it a great choice for use on deer and pronghorn at extreme ranges, and while the Scirocco works equally well on deer, its stouter construction makes it a better choice for heavier game.

The 130-grain Scirocco has a ballistic coefficient of .571, which is higher than most big game bullets regardless of caliber.

There are not many game animals in North America that cannot be taken cleanly with a 130-grain bullet, but anytime I think an upcoming hunt might demand the use of something heavier, I switch to my Rifles Inc. Model 700 in 6.5 STW (which drives a 140-grain bullet at 3,300 fps) or to a larger caliber.

So which of the 6.5mm cartridges is the best? I will tell you which I am most fond of, but they may not be the very best choices for someone else.

For starters, I have a soft spot for the ancient old 6.5x54 Mannlicher-Schoenauer, not because it is necessarily the best of the lot but because of the rifle it has long been associated with. Each time I pick up my trim little Model 1909 Mannlicher-Schoenauer carbine I can envision myself chasing chamois in the Alps.

I also like the 6.5x55 Swedish. Its light recoil makes it fun to shoot, it has been accurate in every rifle in which I have tried it, and it kills deer like a bolt from the blue. (Incidentally, years ago

I designed a wildcat, the 6.5x52, to get 6.5 Swede performance out of a short-action cartridge. It was the 7mm-08 Remington case necked down and fireformed to minimum body taper and a 40-degree shoulder angle. It predates the 7mm-08 and could also be described as an improved version of that cartridge.)

I have also become extremely fond of the 6.5-284 Norma. Its recoil is only slighter heavier than that of the 6.5 Swede, it shoots a bit flatter, hits a bit harder, and I have to try really hard to make it shoot groups larger than an inch from a good rifle. It is also one of the deadliest deer cartridges I have ever used.

For a short-action bolt gun I will have to go with the 6.5

EXTERIOR BALLISTICS, SWIFT 130-GRAIN SCIROCCO (.571 BC)					
	Muzzle	100 yd.	200 yd.	300 yd.	400 yd.
Velocity (fps)	2,900	2,734	2,575	2,421	2,272
Energy (ft.-lbs.)	2,425	2,155	1,912	1,692	1,488
Trajectory (in.)	—	+3.0	+2.8	-2.6	-14.0
Velocity (fps)	3,100	2,927	2,760	2,600	2,445
Energy (ft.-lbs.)	2,771	2,470	2,196	1,949	1,724
Trajectory (in.)	—	+3.0	+3.4	-1.0	-10.0
Velocity (fps)	3,400	3,216	3,038	2,867	2,703
Energy (ft.-lbs.)	3,333	2,982	2,661	2,370	2,107
Trajectory (in.)	—	+3.0	+4.1	+1.5	-5.3

Creedmoor as my pick of the litter. It is quite accurate in the Ruger Model 77 Hawkeye and even more so in my heavy-barrel target rifle. On top of that, in a 26-inch barrel Hornady's Superformance ammo pushes the 120-grain GMX bullet along at an honest 3,100 fps, and the 129-grain SST moves out at just over 2,900 fps.

My last choice is an old wildcat called the 6.5-06. Easily formed by necking down the .30-06 case, it is capable of duplicating the performance of the 6.5-284 Norma and the 6.5 Remington Magnum. I do not find it to be as accurate as the 6.5-284, but that could be the fault of the rifles I have tried it in. For all-around use on deer-size game in open country, its heavier bullet makes it a tad better than the .25-06 and just as good as the .270 Winchester.

BY CRAIG BODDINGTON

THE LIGHT BRIGADE

THREE NON-MAGNUM 7MMS THAT GET THE JOB DONE WITH NO MUSS, NO FUSS.

While it's not the author's favorite cartridge, Steve Hornady (r.) loves the .280 Remington and has used it to kill mountain game across the world such as this Dagestan tur.

The 7mm Remington Magnum has been the most popular belted magnum in the world. It seems to be slipping a bit right now, perhaps somewhat due to both confusion and competition from short magnums (7mm WSM and 7mm Short Action Ultra Mag) and longer, faster magnums (7mm STW and 7mm Ultra Mag). You can add in the 7mm Weatherby Magnum, the new 7mm Blaser Magnum and also proprietary rounds such as the 7mm Dakota Magnum and Lazzeroni's 7.21 (.284) Fireball. In short, there's a very extensive list of "magnum" 7mm cartridges.

In actual fact, none of the fast 7mms are burning up the world in popularity right now. All have their fans, and well they should. They are indeed fast and effective, with the benefits of the 7mm's traditionally long-for-caliber bullets with high sectional densities and high ballistic coefficients. I have used most of the fast 7mms and have never found them wanting, but if I want that level of performance I tend to lean toward the .30 calibers. I do concede that you have to put up with about 20 percent more recoil to get similar trajectory performance from a .30 caliber. But, hey, I'm a heavy bullet guy, and I believe in frontal area, so if I want what we think of as "magnum performance" I choose the fast .30s over the fast 7mms.

However, most of the time we don't need maximum velocity and downrange energy. There is much to be said for simple efficiency: adequate velocity, flat enough trajectory, good bullet performance, adequate energy and moderate recoil. For cartridges that work on a wide range of game under a wide range of conditions—without beating you to death—it's pretty hard to beat what I like to call the "light" 7mms.

There are actually quite a few of these, but I'm going to narrow it down to the three that I think make sense. I discount the 7-30 Waters because it lacks the velocity and power, and I rule out the .284 Winchester because it's no longer chambered in any new rifles. Similarly, the 7x64 Brenneke also doesn't make sense because it's nearly identical in performance to the .280 Remington but with much more limited ammunition availability.

That leaves us with three light 7mms that are worthy of consideration: 7x57 Mauser, 7mm-08 Remington and .280 Remington. All three are superb hunting cartridges; all offer versatile performance over a wide range of conditions; and all offer the genuine benefits of the 7mm (.284) bullet diameter.

None of them deliver heavy recoil, especially in relation to the performance they offer. As we will see, there are considerable overlaps in velocity and performance, so I think it is best to discuss them in the chronological order in which they were introduced.

7x57 MAUSER

Developed by Mauser in 1892, the 7x57 (a.k.a. 7mm Mauser) is one of the oldest smokeless cartridges still in production, and it is definitely the oldest that still has a significant following among hunters here and elsewhere.

It was adopted by Spain in 1893, so Americans were introduced to it during the Spanish-American War in 1898. We won most of the battles, although at considerable cost as we found the 7x57 superior to our .30-40 Krag.

The British were introduced to it at about the same time, during the Second Boer War. They didn't win all the battles either, and although the firepower of their 10-shot .303s beat the Boers' Mausers, they also learned grim lessons about the long-range accuracy of the 7x57.

The 7x57 has always had, and still retains, a modest but loyal following in the United States. After 1925 it gave a lot of ground to the .270 Winchester, and in recent years it has been largely supplanted by the shorter-cased 7mm-08 Remington.

It actually has two problems. First, most modern factory loads are extremely conservative due to concerns over use in pre-1898 Mauser actions. "Standard" today is a 140-grain bullet at an unimpressive 2,660 fps.

Second, by today's standards the 7x57 has an odd case length of 2.244 inches, which is too long for a short bolt action (.308 length, 2.015 inches) but a very loose fit in a standard (.30-06 length, 2.5 inches) bolt action. So you can't have a 7x57 in a short action, and you're wasting magazine space in a .30-06-length action.

These issues aside, I make no bones about it: The 7x57 is far and away my favorite of the light 7mms. It is a wonderfully nostalgic cartridge. Its British designation of .275 Rigby was a favorite of Walter "Karamoja" Bell. The 7x57 was an early favorite of Jack O'Connor (pre-.270), and it remained Eleanor O'Connor's favorite throughout her own hunting career, which certainly rivaled her husband's.

There are a few pretty good factory loads out there. Hornady's Light Magnum had a 140-grain bullet at 2,830 fps, and while that load is no longer cataloged, there are two Superformance loads: a 139-grain SST at 2,760 and a 139-grain GMX at 2,740. Norma has a 156-grain load that runs at 2,641.

In general, however, the 7x57 should be considered primarily a handloader's cartridge today. In handloads it does have greater case capacity than the 7mm-08, so it can be loaded to equal or exceed any 7mm-08. With its greater case capacity, it also does better than the 7mm-08 with heavier bullets.

However it is loaded, it goes about its business with calm efficiency. On game it seems to perform far beyond its seemingly mild ballistics. In part this is because its modest velocity delivers exceptionally good bullet performance—and, undoubtedly, we Americans generally tend toward more velocity and energy than we really need. With decent loads it is easily a 300-yard

One criticism Boddington has regarding the 7x57 is a general lack of accuracy. It's adequate for what most people use it for, but tack drivers in this cartridge are, in his experience, rare.

cartridge, and I think of it as one of our very best deer cartridges and certainly adequate for game up to elk.

It is, of course, much more versatile than that. I have used it literally around the world, taking game such as greater kudu, red stag, Himalayan tahr and a whole lot more. With its original 173-grain full metal jacket roundnose, Karamoja Bell used it to take a large number of the 1,011 elephants he is credited with. I have no interest in stretching its envelope quite that far, but in 2008 I did use it to brain a huge water buffalo with a 175-grain Barnes solid.

I must admit that I have never found the 7x57 to be dramatically accurate, but it has consistently provided adequate accuracy for its sensible range envelope. The

7x57 I have now is a custom rifle made by Todd Ramirez along the lines of a 1920s vintage "stalking rifle." It is thus a nostalgic cartridge in a traditional platform. I love it and use it as often as I can, most recently to take the inaugural deer on my little farm in Kansas.

.280 REMINGTON

The .280 Remington could very possibly be the best of all the factory 7mm cartridges, and it probably is the best factory cartridge based on the .30-06 case. Despite this, it has never been especially popular, probably because both the .270 and the .30-06 were firmly entrenched when it came along, and it pretty much splits the difference between them.

I know that in my own case, when given a choice I generally

Karamoja Bell used the original 173-grain solid in the 7x57 to take hundreds of elephant in the early years of the 20th century, so it's not like the cartridge is underpowered.

prefer either the .270 or the .30-06 over the .280, but this preference isn't based on logic or empirical evidence; it's just not possible to love all cartridges.

The fans of the .280 know how good it is, though. The .280 shoots flatter than the .30-06, and thanks to the aerodynamic qualities of 7mm bullets, shoots as flat as the .270 Winchester but is able to deliver a heavier bullet.

One other possible reason the .280 never achieved huge popularity is because when it was introduced in 1957, the original loads were fairly mild compared to the .270 (and even the .30-06) to ensure reliability in Remington's Model 740 semiautomatic—the first rifle in which it was chambered.

Standard loads today include a 140-grain bullet at 3,050 fps, 150-grain bullet at 2,890 fps, and 165-grain bullet at 2,820 fps. These

are very credible velocities, but due to the cartridge's limited popularity, the selection is fairly limited.

So, like the 7x57, the .280 Remington is at its best as a handloader's cartridge. With good handloads the cartridge comes very close to 7mm Remington Magnum performance—and does it in a shorter barrel while burning a whole lot less powder.

The fans of the .280 Remington are not legion, but they tend to be loyal and steadfast. Among their numbers are Jim Carmichel, longtime and recently retired shooting editor of *Outdoor Life*; the same magazine's editor, Todd Smith; and Steve Hornady.

As I admitted, I am not huge fan, but I have used the .280 here and there. Most recently I had an Ultra Light Arms rifle in .280 Remington, and it shot like a house afire.

I took it on a deer hunt in western Oklahoma, and the only chance I had was on a buck that stepped out of the mist on an adjacent ridge. It was too foggy for the rangefinder to work, so I guesstimated it the old-fashioned way, something over 300 yards but probably not farther than 350, and I gave the buck a backline hold. The Ballistic Silvertip thumped home perfectly, and the buck rolled down the ridge.

With higher velocity and at least equal accuracy, the .280 is better-suited to open country than either of the other two cartridges we are discussing. With its ability to use heavier bullets at higher velocities, it is also better for larger game such as elk. The only real negative I can give it is that it generates more recoil than the other two 7mm cartridges.

7mm-08 REMINGTON

The 7mm-08 Remington was introduced in 1980, so it's a relatively new cartridge. Unlike the other two, its factory loads have been loaded to the gills from the starting gate. Based on a .308 Winchester case necked down, it's a perfect fit in a short bolt action, yet there are no flies on its performance, especially with 140-grain bullets. The standard 140-grain load runs at 2,800 fps, with some loads a little faster.

Because of limited case capacity it does start to lose velocity with heavier bullets; the 150-grain factory load is standard at 2,650 fps, which is quite a bit of velocity loss for a gain of just 10 grains in bullet weight.

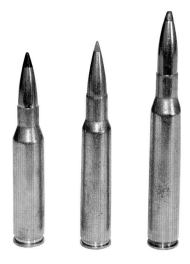

Left to right: 7mm-08 Remington, 7x57 Mauser, .280 Remington. These "light" 7mms offer hunters most everything they need—without everything they don't, such as blast and recoil.

it cannot be housed in a short-action rifle.

I'm not altogether sure I have ever taken a single game animal with a 7mm-08. However, I've shot plenty enough game with the 7x57 to know what a 140-grain 7mm bullet at plus or minus 2,800 fps will do; what a 150-grain 7mm bullet between 2,600 and 2,700 fps will do; what a 160- to 165-grain 7mm bullet at 2,500 to 2,600 fps will do; and what a 175-grain 7mm bullet at 2,300 to 2,400 fps will do.

Unless you have a strong desire to emulate Walter Bell, the 7mm-08—with its greater selection of factory loads and ability to be housed in a shorter, lighter rifle—makes far more sense than a 7x57.

Recoil is delightfully mild, and at the modest velocity, good bullet performance is almost assured. It is not a long-range cartridge, but it also not a short-

However, our modern hunting bullets are so good that there are relatively few sensible things that you can't do with a good 140-grain 7mm bullet.

The first time I ever saw a 7mm-08 used on game was when I hunted with Chub Eastman, then of Nosler Bullets, in 1980 or '81. I guess I was in the latter phase of my magnum mania, so I thought his 7mm-08 seemed awfully small for a big boar. He took a broadside shot on a big hog at about 100 yards, and the bullet whistled through both shoulders and exited. I was impressed, and my respect for the little 7mm-08 has never diminished.

Now, in real terms, the 7mm-08 and the 7x57 are indistinguishable in their effects on game. If you shoot factory loads, the 7mm-08 has a clear edge over the Mauser, and certainly it has the ability to fit into a short action, with the benefits of a shorter, lighter, and handier rifle. With good handloads the 7x57 is superior, but as I mentioned,

CARTRIDGE COMPARISON
THE LIGHT BRIGADE

Cartridge/Load	Bullet Weight (gr.)	Muzzle Velocity (fps)	Muzzle Energy (ft.-lbs.)	300-Yd. Drop (in.)*
7x57 Mauser				
Federal Nosler Partition	140	2,660	2,200	-9.0
Remington Core-Lokt	140	2,660	2,199	-9.4
Norma Oryx	156	2,641	2,417	-10.0
7mm-08 Remington				
Remington Nosler Partition	140	2,860	2,542	-7.5
Federal Nosler Ballistic Tip	140	2,800	2,440	-8.4
Federal Speer Hot-Cor	150	2,650	2,340	-9.2
.280 Remington				
Federal Nosler AccuBond	140	3,000	2,800	-6.5
Winchester Ballistic Silvertip	140	3,040	2,872	-6.3
Remington Core-Lokt	165	2,820	2,913	-9.1
FOR COMPARISON				
7mm Rem. Mag.				
Remington Core-Lokt Ultra	140	3,175	3,085	-6.0
Remington Core-Lokt	150	3,110	3,221	-6.6

*200-yard zero

range cartridge. The 7mm-08 will reach handily to at least 300 yards and in my experience tends to be more accurate on average than the 7x57.

It's a great cartridge for the seasoned hunter who likes to do his work with maximum efficiency and minimum fuss, and to my thinking it is the best choice of all for a beginning hunter.

It is far more capable—but produces only slightly more recoil—than the .243 Winchester most of us start our kids with, and for that reason when my daughter Britanny turned 17 and wanted to take up hunting, there was no doubt in my mind what centerfire cartridge she should start with: the 7mm-08.

ALL HAIL THE .308

By Craig Boddingto

The author grudgingly admits the .30-06's little brother has a lot going for it.

A very wise man once said, "You can't please all the people all the time." In my business, well, you really can't win. I am an unabashed fan of the .30-06 Springfield. It is impossible to love all cartridges equally, especially cartridges that are similar in performance. So I've never been a big fan of the .308 Winchester, and I freely admit that there have been many times when I gave it shorter shrift than I might have.

Eventually tiring of reader mail chiding me for, at worst, ignoring the .308 or, perhaps at best, damning it with faint praise, I made a conscious decision that when writing about things like non-magnum .30s and versatile hunting cartridges I would do my best to give the .308 its proper due—even though it wasn't my "thing."

One of the comments I have made, and I believe this to be absolutely true, is that, on average, the .308 Winchester is a more accurate cartridge than the .30-06 Springfield. Like I said, you can't win. This garnered me a really snippy letter, I suppose from a .30-06 fan, who challenged this statement and asked what I based it on and if I had proved it through proper testing.

No, I have not. Although I much prefer the .30-06, I have long accepted as gospel that the .308 is, on average, a more accurate cartridge. I accept it to the degree that attempting to prove it seems a lot like trying to prove that a Ferrari is faster than a Volkswagen, although the degree is much less. Realistically, however, it is far beyond my capability or interest to try to prove this quantitatively. In theory I could order, say, 100 similar bolt-action rifles in each caliber (.30-06 in a standard-length action, .308 in a short-action version) and 1,000 rounds of a good match load in each cartridge and group each rifle. I'd be broke long before I finished, but I fervently believe the .308 would be the winner.

The cartridge we now know as the 7.62mm NATO or .308 Winchester was designed after World War II as a replacement for the .30-06 in America's service rifle and light and medium machine guns. It was created by a fairly simple shortening and re-necking of the .30-06 case, resulting in a case that is about a third of an inch shorter.

This considerably reduces powder capacity, which must result in somewhat lower velocity. The military was willing to make this trade. For many years, the .30-06 had ruled as the world's most powerful standard military cartridge, so there was a bit of wiggle room there. Also, propellant powders in the 1950s were quite a lot better than in the early years of smokeless powder, when the .30-06 was developed.

When the .308 was introduced as a civilian cartridge in 1952, and when finally adopted by the military two years later, it was not as fast as the .30-06. Powders are even better today, and the gap has narrowed, but the .308 will never be as fast a cartridge as the .30-06. However, its shorter case is more efficient,

which is why the velocity gap is as narrow as it is.

The primary advantage for the military was that the shorter cartridge could be more easily housed in more compact and efficient semiautomatic and automatic actions. The ammunition would be lighter, and the 20-round magazines for what became the M14 would be lighter and more easily carried than the bulky, cumbersome magazines for the heavy, cumbersome Browning Automatic Rifle.

For 50 years, the .30-06 had been legendary for long-range accuracy, especially in the beloved Springfield, so I don't believe enhanced accuracy was on anyone's radar screen. It is, however, a byproduct of the shorter, more efficient case.

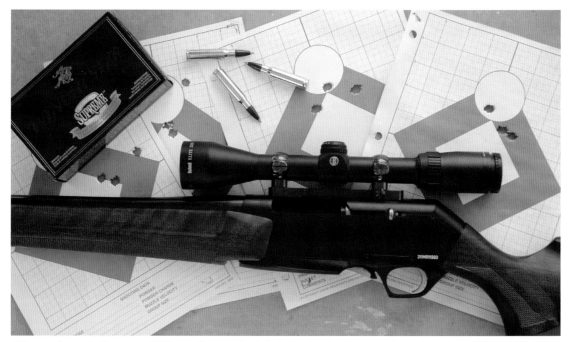

Rifles such as the Browning BAR are often available in both short and long actions. The short-action .308 will, of course, be a bit lighter and more compact than the exact same rifle in .30-06.

For the last dozen years we've had this beaten into our heads as a benefit of the short magnums. We didn't hear about this much in the 1950s when the .308 was new, but this was fact then and remains fact today: The greater the percentage of the powder column instantly ignited by the primer flame, the smoother the burning curve. More energy is developed per grain of powder burned (again, this is why the velocity gap between the two cartridges is as narrow as it is), and this same burning efficiency is conducive to more consistent accuracy.

The other accuracy advantage held by the .308 is that shorter actions are more rigid. Now, if a .308 Winchester is housed in a .30-06-length action that simply has a shorter magazine box, this

The .308 was created by simply shortening the .30-06 case and re-necking. Despite their size difference, their ballistic performances are surprisingly similar.

advantage doesn't exist. But if a .308 is housed in a shorter action designed for the cartridge length, then that action is more rigid and flexes less during firing. It is another simple fact that this is conducive to better and more consistent accuracy.

So in any head-to-head test of a group of .308 rifles versus similar .30-06 rifles, I believe the on-average accuracy winner will always be the .308. On the other hand, quality of barrel, precision of bedding and assembly, and that weird anomaly of harmonics between load and rifle are all more important to accuracy than cartridge design and rigidity of action.

The .30-06 is an accurate cartridge. Many individual .30-06 rifles will outshoot individual .308 rifles, and it isn't unthinkable that in any test of a group of rifles in each cartridge a .30-06 could come as the single most accurate individual rifle, but on average the .308 should win.

There are slide, lever, bolt, break-open, falling block and self-loading actions chambered to both cartridges. Single-shots excepted, it takes more steel to house a .30-06 cartridge than a .308, and in the case of semi-autos and the rare .30-06 lever action such as Browning's long-action BLR, it takes more engineering—but it can be done.

I have never paid much attention to—and have little experience with—the advantages of short actions because they're rarely made for lefties like me. But the simple fact is short actions are not only more rigid, they are also

lighter and more compact, and with a repeating action genuinely sized to the shorter cartridge, the operating stroke is shorter—thus at least theoretically faster and less prone to error.

A shorter, lighter and more compact action is a definite advantage, so this one has to go to the .308. As for faster and more goof-proof, well, I'm pretty fast with a left-handed bolt gun regardless of action length. I've never short-stroked a bolt action (though I've seen it done many times), but in all my years I have used just two genuine short-action left-handed bolt guns. Both Remington and Winchester made a handful for a brief time, and I've had one of each: a Model 70 in .270 WSM and an MGA in .350 Remington Magnum based on a short left-hand Model 700 action. Both rifles are fast, but I don't have enough experience with left-handed short actions to have a firm opinion.

Instead, I will defer to one of the greatest bolt-action men of all time, Walter Dalrymple Maitland "Karamoja" Bell, who took the vast majority of his 1,011 elephants with bolt-action rifles in calibers much smaller than we recommend today. In one of his last stories, written after the introduction of the .308 Winchester, he wrote that if he could start over, his concept of the perfect rifle for harvesting ivory (which is not the same as trophy hunting) would be a short bolt-action in .308 Winchester loaded with 220-grain solids.

Velocity would obviously be fairly low, possibly 2,250 fps, but

While neither the .308 nor the '06 are great for high mountain hunts, they're both excellent deer rounds—and the .308 is handier while not sacrificing a whole lot in terms of ballistics.

nobody knew better than Bell how much velocity is required to overcome resistance in order to penetrate. More to the point, he saw the short bolt throw made possible by the .308 as a decided advantage over the Enfields, Mannlichers and Mausers that he used chambered in .303 British, 6.5x53R, 6.5x54, 7x57 and .318 Westley-Richards. I cannot dispute such authority: The .308 in an action sized for the cartridge scores another point.

And then there's the recoil question. Since the .308 develops slightly more energy per grain of powder burned, and since with standard hunting weight bullets it will always lag a minimum of 80 to a maximum of maybe 120 fps behind the '06, it produces less recoil. This is irrefutable physics. On the other hand, this is probably evened out by the

fact that, in short actions, .308 sporters should be a bit lighter than near-identical rifles in .30-06. Lighter rifles produce more recoil.

So I don't buy that the .308 offers a lighter-recoiling option to the .30-06. And even if it does, the difference isn't significant. Both cartridges are powerful rounds producing energy one side or the other of 3,000 ft.-lbs. Neither generate magnum-level recoil, but neither can be considered mild-recoiling cartridges.

While I am a .30-06 fan, I don't claim a lifelong allegiance to it. Like so many riflemen of my generation and the two generations that preceded me, my first centerfire rifle was a surplus Springfield, but I didn't hunt with that rifle when I was a kid.

The first time I used the cartridge was on my first African sa-

fari in 1977. Man, it worked great! With 180-grain Nosler Partitions loaded to 2,800 fps it performed like Thor's hammer. I have used many other cartridges since, including the .308 Winchester, but with so many cartridges that actually offer relatively similar performance on game, it really comes down to confidence. In situations where the range is unlikely to be extreme, I have supreme confidence in the .30-06, and I have never achieved this confidence level with the .308.

I admit this is silly. My dad took almost all of his game— moose, bear, deer, pronghorn and more—with a Winchester M70 in .308. He had supreme confidence in the .308, the kind of confidence I have in the .30-06, and neither of us is wrong because the ballistic differences are so slight.

.308 vs. .30-06 BALLISTICS

Cartridge	Bullet	Bullet Weight (gr.)	Muzzle Velocity (fps)	Muzzle Energy (ft.-lbs.)	300 yd. Drop** (in.)	Wind Drift (in.)		
						100 yd.	200 yd.	300 yd.
.308	Hornady Custom SST	150	2,820	2,648	-7.9	0.6	2.5	5.8
.30-06	Hornady Custom SST	150	2,910	2,820	-7.4	0.6	2.4	5.5
.308	Hornady Superformance SST	150	3,000	2,997	-6.9	0.5	2.2	5.3
.30-06	Hornady Superformance SST	150	3,080	3,159	-6.4	0.5	2.1	5.0
.308	Hornady SST*	165	2,700	2,670	-8.6	0.6	5.4	5.5
.30-06	Hornady Custom SST	165	2,800	2,872	-7.9	0.5	2.2	5.2
.308	Hornady Superformance SST	165	2,840	2,955	-7.9	0.5	2.2	5.1
.30-06	Hornady Superformance SST	165	2,960	3,209	-6.9	0.5	2.0	4.8
.308	Hornady SST*	180	2,500	2,498	-10	0.6	2.5	5.8
.30-06	Hornady Custom SST	180	2,700	2,913	-8.4	0.5	2.2	5.1
.30-06	Hornady Superformance	180	2,820	3,178	-7.6	0.5	2.1	4.9

Notes: (*Handload) (**200-yard zero)

Realistically, the differences are slight. Today's 180-grain .30-06 load is "standard" at 2,700 fps; 180-grain .308 loads run about 2,612. Energy runs maybe 150 ft.-lbs. less, and the difference in trajectory at 300 yards is less than an inch. Neither cartridge is a particularly good choice for much longer shooting.

With heavier bullets case capacity really starts to tell. The .308 falls off quickly with 200- or 220-grain bullets, but realistically we're not wading into elephant herds with .30 caliber rifles. Our hunting bullets are so much better today that there is little necessity for a .30 caliber bullet over 180 grains. I do prefer a 180-grain bullet for elk, bears and the run of African plains game, but one could argue that, with modern bullets, you can go a bit lighter and achieve the same results. In the .308 or .30-06, 150-grain bullets are perfect for any deer-size game, and 165-grain bullets are a fine compromise for darn near

anything these cartridges are suited for.

With 150- or 165-grain bullets, thanks to modern powders and the .308's case efficiency, the performance gap is pretty narrow. The 150-grain .30-06 runs about 2,910 fps in standard factory loads; the 165-grain bullet runs about 2,800. The 150-grain .308 is standard at 2,820 fps, while the 165-grain load averages about 2,700 fps. So, pretty much across the board with bullets up to 180 grains the .308 is about 100 fps slower than the .30-06. This is about three or four percent, which is not significant.

In all cases velocity can be increased somewhat by judicious handloading, and there are faster factory loads out there such as Hornady's Superformance load, but the performance differential remains pretty much the same— although there is no 180-grain Superformance .308 load, which suggests that, because of case capacity, they couldn't get the

velocity up enough to make it worth the trouble.

As much as I hate to admit it, I have to concede that the .308 is the better cartridge. Ballistics are too close to argue about, and whether it's mostly theoretical or actual, the .308 should have the accuracy edge. Perhaps most importantly, it will fit into more actions, and actions that are lighter and more compact.

Field use? Identical. Neither are good long-cartridges, so they're not ideal for mountain game or wide-open plains. Neither are good choices for big bears or larger dangerous game. Both are wonderful deer cartridges, fully adequate for elk and black bear, and plenty versatile enough for African plains game.

Take your pick. Given a choice, I'll stick with the .30-06, but if you choose the .308 instead, well, you're probably right.

The
LOWER
FORTY

by Craig Boddington

THE WORLD OF THE "LARGE MEDIUM" .40 CALIBER HAS MORE VARIETY AND UTILITY THAN YOU MIGHT THINK.

Veteran shooters love to throw around terms intended to baffle beginners and make them think we possess not just experience but a wealth of knowledge. For instance, "big bore." That's not a fat old guy like me who keeps repeating himself but a large-caliber cartridge.

Is there a precise definition for this? In the blackpowder era, bores between .40 and .50 were considered medium bores, with the big bores usually designated by gauge (round lead balls to the pound) rather than caliber. In the smokeless era, calibers over .450 inch were considered big bores.

Thanks to the British gun trade's proprietary system, all the major gun

makers had their own cartridges, which they sold along with the rifles at a handy profit. So there were lots of British big bores from .450 and up.

There were also a few great cartridges between .400 and .450. In *African Rifles and Cartridges*, John Taylor dubbed these "large mediums"—certainly apt in a global sense, but in North America we must consider them way above medium. Our largest land mammal, the bison, can be hunted with a .30 caliber and good bullets. We do have the largest bears on the planet, both white and brown, and they are formidable. But a lot of hunters use .30 calibers with good bullets, and long-established wisdom says the .338s and .375s are just fine for the largest bears.

In the late 1950s and early '60s, as Great Britain got out of the empire business, the demand for large-caliber cartridges diminished, and the old big bores were discontinued. Enter the brash Americans with their relatively inexpensive .375 bolt rifles (first the Winchester Model 70, introduced in 1937) and also the upstart .458 Win. Mag. cartridge. When I started hunting in Africa in the mid-1970s, these two cartridges were just about all that you saw.

Forgive the heresy, but the .416 Rigby was not a popular cartridge. It was retained by Rigby as a proprietary round, so only a few hundred Rigby rifles were ever made. Add in a few dozen continental and American custom rifles, and that's the world production from 1911 to 1988.

It was, however, a great and effective cartridge with a reputation—actually legend—that far exceeded its actual use. Robert Ruark wrote about it, and Jack O'Connor owned and used one. It refused to die. Bullets and cases were scarce, but enterprising American handloaders fixed that.

The .416 Taylor, the .458 Win. Mag. case necked down to .416, was a popular wildcat in the late 1970s. Designed by gun writer Robert Chatfield-Taylor, the .416 Taylor almost made it into factory form at least twice, and the only reason it didn't, I think, is the feeling that Americans didn't need (and thus wouldn't buy) such a powerful cartridge. After all, the .458 was selling far better than it should, so why dilute limited success?

For some years, Barnes bullets and RCBS dies had kept the .416 alive, and the belts could be turned off .460 Wby. brass to make .416 Rigby cases. But by this time there were more bullets and new .416 Rigby cases from Jim Bell's Brass Extrusion Laboratories Limited.

The .416 Taylor was still out there, the .416 Hoffman (an improved .375 H&H case necked up to .416 by African professional hunter and American expat George Hoffman in the 1980s) was a popular wildcat, and the .416 Rigby was experiencing a rebirth in custom rifles. The handwriting was on the wall: the .416 was coming back.

The rebirth came between 1988 and 1989. Remington adapted (rather than adopted) the .416 Hoffman, changing the shoulder and body taper slightly by using its own 8mm Rem. Mag. case to create the .416 Rem. Mag. Within months Federal offered the first American factory load for the .416 Rigby, and Bill Ruger had a magnum version of his Model 77 in .416 Rigby, a cartridge he had long admired. Weatherby quickly countered with the .416 Wby. Mag., the belted .460 case necked down to .416—and, of course, loaded to the gills.

Standard and traditional .416 Rigby ballistics were a 410-grain bullet at 2,370 fps. Rounding bullet weight down and velocity up, most common today is a 400-grain bullet at 2,400 fps, an energy yield of just over 5,000 ft.-lbs. The Taylor with its reduced case capacity came close, and these are the basic figures for the .416 Hoffman and .416 Rem. Mag. However, with its greater case capacity the .416 Rigby can be loaded much hotter, all the way up to the 400-grain bullet at 2,600 fps of the .416 Wby.

Mag. Performance is awesome, but recoil becomes ferocious.

One limitation was that the .416s were all rimless and belted rimless cartridges best-suited for bolt-action rifles. Krieghoff fixed that in the 1990s with the first and only modern Nitro Express cartridge, the .500/.416 3.25-inch Nitro Express, a big rimmed cartridge designed for double rifles. As such it's not a huge

seller, but it offers .416 performance and capability in the two-pipe rifle. Velocity is reduced slightly to 2,350 fps to reduce pressure, but no game animal is going to notice the 50 fps difference.

Although there are other wildcat and proprietary .416s, this was the status quo for factory .416 for nearly 20 years. Then in 2008 Hornady necked up the .375 Ruger case to create the .416 Ruger. Ballistics are, once again, essentially the same as the .416 Rigby's 1911 numbers, except that, like the wildcat .416 Taylor, the .416 Ruger can be housed in a .30-06-length action and is available in the Model 77 Hawkeye.

So where do these rounds fit in the scheme of things? The .416 pretty much splits the difference between the .375 and .450 calibers. While they're popular, I don't think the .416s have created a new market of their own but have simply stolen market share from both the .375s and the true big bores.

The true big bores are almost useless for North American hunting, and except for the big bears there is no real justification for a "large medium" such as the .416. However, if you have a .416 and really want to use it,

Although not easy to shoot well, the large mediums tend to be extremely accurate. Shown here is a composite group of Hornady's 400-grain DGX expanding bullet and DGS solid out of a Ruger M77 Hawkeye Alaskan in .416 Ruger.

LOWER .40 COMPARISON

Cartridge	Bullet Diameter (in.)	Manufacturer/ Bullet	Bullet Weight (gr.)	Muzzle Velocity (fps)	Muzzle Energy (ft.-lbs.)
.405 Win.	.411	Hornady Interlock	300	2,200	3,224
.450/.400 3-in. Nitro	.410*	Hornady DGX	400	2,050	3,732
.500/.416 3.25-in. Nitro	.416	Norma Woodleigh	410	2,325	4,922
.416 Ruger	.416	Hornady DGX	400	2,400	5,115
.416 Rem. Mag.	.416	Remington Swift A-Frame	400	2,400	5,115
.416 Rigby	.416	Federal Trophy Bonded BC	400	2,300	4,698
.416 Rigby	.416	Hornady DGX	400	2,400	5,115
.416 Rigby	.416	Norma Woodleigh	450	2,150	4,620
.404 Jeffery	.423	McMillan North Fork SS	400	2,300	4,698
.404 Jeffery	.423	Norma Woodleigh	450	2,150	4,620
.425 Westley Richards	.435	Kynoch Woodleigh	410	2,350	5,010
.416 Wby. Mag.	.416	Weatherby Barnes TSX	400	2,700	6,474

NOTES: *The .450/.400 was offered by many manufacturers and varies considerably in exact bore diameter in older rifles; the variance is generally as tight as .408 and as generous as .412. Hornady's compromise of .410 should be safe in rifles in sound condition but may not provide optimum accuracy in some older rifles with extreme bore variation. Abbreviations: BC, Bear Claw; SS, semi-spitzer

These British large mediums are again available. While the .416 Rigby (r.) got all the glory, the .404 Jeffery (l.) and .425 Westley Richards (c.) were actually more popular.

velocity is high enough and trajectory flat enough that you can make it work.

In Africa the situation is a bit different, but perhaps not as different as you think. The .375 remains the benchmark minimum for dangerous game, maybe a bit dicey for elephant in close cover, but okay for buffalo, perfect for lion and extremely versatile for use on plains game. The true big bores are definitely better for elephant and a bit better for buffalo, but even there they are specialized, lacking the trajectory and (traditionally) the sighting equipment for plains game and even lion.

Enter the large medium. On smaller game the .416 is not as versatile as the .375, but it is far more versatile than a big bore. On larger game, because of its higher velocity the .416s have energy yields (5,000 ft.-lbs.) similar to the big bores but because of smaller bullet diameter actually penetrate better. I will not suggest that the .416s are as dramatically effective as a .458 Lott or .500 Nitro Express, but there is no animal they can't kill, and they are definitely more decisive than any .375.

I started with a .416 Hoffman in the mid-1980s, and since then I have used pretty much all of the .416s. It

is impossible to choose better or best among them; it depends on which rifle you like and which ammo source you prefer. All are readily available today, but no manufacturer loads them all.

Interestingly, the world of large mediums is no longer strictly a .416 world. Actually, it never was. Among the rimmed cartridges for single-shots and double rifles the .470 got the glory, but the most popular by far was the milder, lighter-recoiling and more versatile .450/.400—a .40 caliber 400-grain bullet at about 2,100 fps for 4,000 ft.-lbs. of energy. In part this is because India was actually a larger market for double rifles than Africa, and the .450/.400 was considered perfect for tiger.

There were two non-interchangeable versions, one with a three-inch case and thicker rim, and the other with a quarter-inch more case length. A few years ago Hornady brought back the .450/.400 3-inch in a modern load. Ruger offers its No. 1 Tropical single-shot in this great old cartridge, and all makers of modern double rifles are offering it as well. It's easy to shoot and offers great penetration. It is not the equal of the faster .416s, but it's perfect for buffalo and makes a great choice in a double-barrel or single-shot.

Similarly, although the .416 Rigby got the glory, the most popular large-medium bore was actually the .404 Jeffery, introduced in 1908. You could even say the third British large medium, the .425 Westley Richards, was more popular than the Rigby cartridge.

The .404 Jeffery was manufactured by numerous makers, and it was standard game department issue in most of Britain's African colonies. Thousands were made, and unlike most large-caliber cartridges, ammunition was always available because RWS never stopped loading it.

Although maintained as a proprietary of Westley Richards, the .425 was adopted as standard issue by the Uganda game department. The .425 Westley Richards is a strange-looking cartridge with a rebated rim and

a very long neck that uses an oddball .435-inch bullet, but its ballistics are similar to the .416 Rigby, so it's a powerful and effective cartridge. Ammunition is available, and Westley Richards still makes rifles, but the .425 is rare today.

On the other hand, the .404 Jeffery is staging a comeback. Ammunition is available from several sources, including Hornady, McMillan and Norma. Unlike the .416 Rigby, which needs a full-up magnum action, the .404 can be housed in a .375-length action (as can the .425).

The .404 Jeffery was designed to replicate .450/.400 ballistics in a bolt action, so the original load was a 400-grain bullet at a fairly mild 2,125 fps, yielding right at 4,000 ft.-lbs. of energy. Like the .450/.400, this is a light-recoiling load that is perfect for buffalo but perhaps marginal for elephant.

The .404 doesn't have the case capacity of the .416 Rigby, but with modern powders it can greatly exceed those original velocities. Most modern .404 loads have a 400-grain bullet at around 2,300 fps. Although recoil is a bit milder, performance is so close to the .416 Rigby and Remington it's not worth arguing about.

We also shouldn't overlook the original American .40, the .405 Winchester—Theodore Roosevelt's "lion medicine." About a decade ago, Ruger chambered the No. 1 to .405 and Hornady brought out (and continues to make) new factory ammo. Begging Roosevelt's pardon, but with its light-for-caliber 300-grain bullet the .405 is not an African cartridge because the performance is limited by the action length of the lever-action Model 95 Winchester.

It is, however, a useful North American cartridge, a real thumper for black bear and wild boar, and awesome for elk and moose in close cover. Cartridge length is not an issue in the Ruger No. 1 nor is action strength. So in a modern single-shot, with 400-grain bullets the .405 can be hopped up to .450/.400 performance.

My daughter Brittany has a Ruger in .405 that she's used on buffalo in

Africa and Australia, and we used 400-grain bullets loaded to 2,100 fps. With standard 300-grain loads the .405 is not a giant killer, but it hits hard and has mild recoil, and the bullets we have for it today are a whole lot better than Teddy had in 1909.

So if you're in the market for a lower .40, what should you choose? The good news is there aren't any wrong

(L.-r.) .500/.416 3.25 Nitro, .416 Ruger, .404 Jeffery, .416 Rem. Mag., .416 Rigby, .416 Wby. Mag. With the exception of the Weatherby—which is much faster and more powerful—these cartridges should be considered identical in performance.

The .404 Jeffery is a great lower .40 that's experiencing a well-deserved comeback. Boddington is shooting it here in a McMillan rifle.

Brittany Boddington took this buffalo with a Ruger No. 1 in .405 Winchester using 400-grain bullets loaded to approximate .450/.400 ballistics—a loading made possible by the strength of the action and lack of OAL limitations.

choices. Of the factory rounds, the .416 Wby. Mag. is the fastest and flattest-shooting, so it's technically the most versatile for the widest range of game. It is also the hardest-recoiling, and not everyone can stand up to it.

At the other end of the spectrum, the .405 Winchester is the mildest of the group. For pure North American use it must not be overlooked, but for African use the rest are better. In double rifles and single-shots the choices are the .450/.400 and .500/.416. The latter is faster, thus perhaps more versatile, but 5,000 ft.-lbs. of energy has an attendant level of recoil. At 4,000 ft.-lbs. the .450/.400 is okay for elephant, outstanding for buffalo and a whole lot more fun to shoot.

Among the bolt-action cartridge, I am a long-time fan of the .416 Rigby, but this is based primarily on tradition. For the same reason—and because it fits in a tidier action—I have become a big fan of the .404 Jeffery.

With modern loads readily available, nostalgia is a perfectly good reason to choose a cartridge, but from a purely pragmatic standpoint, the lower .40s that make the most sense are the .416 Rem. Mag. and .416 Ruger. Ballistics are essentially the same as the .416 Rigby and .404 Jeffery (with modern loads), but rifles and ammo are cheaper, rifles are more available, and ammo availability today is pretty much the same across the board.

By Layne Simpson

.50 FOR THE LAST FRONTIER

The .50 B&M Alaskan is a lever-action cartridge just right for big browns and mean moose.

The author tested .50 B&M Alaskan loads with (from l.) 300-grain Hornady FTX, 325-grain Swift A-Frame, 350-grain Speer Deep Curl, 400-grain Sierra JSP, 400-grain Barnes Buster, and 500-grain Hornady XTP flatpoint.

B ack in the 1950s, Cooper Landing, Alaska, gunsmith Harold Johnson decided to neck up the .348 Winchester case for .458-inch bullets and create a powerful big game cartridge for use in lever-action rifles. He called it the .450 Alaskan, and it had a powder capacity slightly greater than that of the .458 Winchester Magnum, which enabled the big cartridge to exceed 2,000 fps with a bullet weighing 400 grains at a chamber pressure level easily handled by two rifles: the smokeless powder version of the Winchester Model 1886 and the Winchester Model 71. Alaska bear guides found the big cartridge to be just the ticket for preventing their clientele from being mauled by a hungry bear or gored by a bull moose in rut.

Then came a .50 caliber version of the same cartridge. As the story goes, Johnson acquired a Winchester Model 86 in .50-110 with a bad barrel and decided to make a replacement for it from a military-surplus machine gun barrel in .50 BMG. But rather than chamber the new barrel for the Winchester cartridge, he necked up the .450 Alaskan case to .50 caliber.

Lacking a jacketed bullet for his new cartridge, Johnson sliced away part of the 750-grain .50 BMG bullet. When shooting his homemade 450-grain bullet base-forward, he claimed it would zip clean through a moose or a brown bear from any angle. Johnson always referred to the cartridge as "the .50," but it eventually became more commonly known as the .50 Alaskan.

The same guys who developed the .50 B&M Alaskan (l.) also came up with (beginning second from l.) the .50 Super Short, .50 SA, .50 B&M and .50 MDM.

The case can be fire-formed using a small charge of Bullseye and an inert filler such as Cream of Wheat breakfast cereal. It can also be formed with a special die set available from RCBS. A third option is to simply buy a supply of .50 Alaskan cases from Starline. Woodleigh offers a 500-grain flatnose bullet of .510-inch diameter made specifically for the cartridge while Buffalo Arms Co. has loaded ammo with both jacketed and cast bullets.

The latest version of this cartridge is the .50 B&M Alaskan, which was named for its developers, William Bruton and Michael McCourry. And when I use the word "developers" here, I mean just that. Hunters of considerable

experience, they thrive on the technical aspect of rifles and cartridges as much as going after big game.

Both are fans of big holes through rifle barrels, and their cartridges of various calibers have given them plenty of excuses to head to Africa on a number of occasions for bullet-testing excursions for elephant, Cape buffalo, hippo and such.

The .50 project started with Bruton's desire for a handy brush rifle of that caliber on the Winchester Model 70 WSSM action. And so was born the .50 B&M Super Short, the case of which was originally formed by shortening and necking up the .300 WSM case. Next in line was a slightly longer version of that cartridge called the .50 SA (semi-auto) designed for the AR-10 rifle made by DPMS.

Then came a medium-length bolt gun cartridge called the .50 B&M and it was followed by a long-action cartridge called the .500 MDM, both on the .404 Jeffrey case. Muzzle velocities range from 1,700 fps with a 500-grain bullet in the .50 Super Short to 2,250 fps for a 550-grain bullet in the .50 MDM. Unprimed brass with proper head-stamping is available from Quality Cartridge.

All those cartridges were developed in custom rifles built by SSK Industries in Wintersville, Ohio. (Bunton and McCourry are not in the "gun business," although they do offer the occasional rifle for sale at their website, b-mriflesandcartridges.com. They steer you to SSK Industries, sskindustries.com, for gun builds.)

Developed for lever-action rifles, the .50 B&M Alaskan case is formed by slightly necking the down Starline .50 Alaskan case so bullets made for the .500 S&W Magnum can be used. A rifling twist rate as slow as 1:20 will stabilize the heaviest of .500 S&W Magnum bullets.

An abundance of readily available .500-inch bullets in weights ranging from 275 to 500 grains gives it a practical edge over the original .50 Alaskan and its .510-inch bullet. In addition, molds are available from Lyman, RCBS, Redding and NEI for casting lead bullets of various weights. Reloading dies are available from RCBS and Hornady.

The Marlin 1895 and Browning Model 71 in .50 B&M Alaskan I shot were converted by SSK Industries and had Pac-Nor barrels. Work performed on the two actions included opening up the loading port a bit and modifying the loading gate and cartridge carrier. And since the replacement barrel is slightly larger in diameter than the factory barrel, the barrel channel in the fore-end and the steel fore-end cap have to be enlarged. The action is then fine-tuned to assure smooth cartridge feeding.

The Model 71 had an 18-inch barrel and weighed 7½ pounds. An XS Systems aperture sight with a .190-inch aperture in a custom base was attached to the top of the receiver. Up front, a banded N.E.C.G. sight held a .100-inch, sourdough-style blade with a gold-colored insert. Attached to the barrel about a third of the way out was an SSK T'SOB base for mounting a long-eye-relief scope.

A quarter-pound lighter than the Model 71, the Marlin 1895 also had an 18-inch barrel. Muzzle diameter was .785 inch compared to .745 inch for the Browning. In comparison, factory .45-caliber Model 1895 barrels range from .720 inch for early production to .740 inch on later rifles. The Marlin rifle wore front and rear sights from N.E.C.G.

It should be noted that at .50 B&M Alaskan impact velocities some of the .500 S&W Magnum bullets are too soft for use on the larger game animals, especially inside 50 yards where velocities are still high. Most would likely work fine on deer, but for bears weighing much over 300 pounds—as well as moose and elk—a stout bullet is in order.

Both the Marlin 1895 (top) and Browning Model 71 conversions to .50 B&M Alaskan were done by SSK Industries.

Dies for the cartridge are available from RCBS, and Alliant offers two powders that are excellent choices.

McCourry has found the 500-grain Hornady at 1,800 to 1,900 fps and a custom SSK 425-grain all-copper hollow-nose bullet at the same velocity to be deadly on game as large as eland and giraffe, with great penetration and weight retention. I think either would work on any game animal in North America, and that includes grizzly out to 125 paces or so, but the ultimate bear medicine for this cartridge may be the upcoming 450-grain bonded-core bullet designed by McCourry and made by North Fork Bullets.

For deer-size game, McCourry likes the 400-grain Sierra Sports Master at 2,000 fps and the 300-grain Hornady FTX at 2,100 fps. Overall cartridge length with the FTX bullet is too long for the Marlin, a problem easily solved by slightly shortening the case. That bullet works fine in the Model 71 with a full-length case.

As powders go, IMR-4198, Reloder 7 and Reloder 10X have proven to be some of the better choices.

On a good day I am capable of staying around an inch at 50 yards with irons, so when shooting the two rifles I stuck with the aperture sight on the Browning and the open sight on the Marlin. The Browning averaged two inches and slightly less with three loads: Swift 325-grain A-frame and 62.0 grains RL-10X for 2,062 fps; Sierra 400-grain JSP and 62.0 gr. IMR-4198 at 2,047 fps; and Hornady 500-grain FP/XTP with 58.0 grains RL-7 at 1,834 fps). The Marlin delivered the same accuracy with the Sierra and Hornady bullets.

Other, less-accurate loads I tried included the Hornady 300-grain FTX with 65.0 grains IMR-4198 at 2,156 fps; Speer 250-grain Deep-Curl with 61.0 grains RL-7 at 1,986 fps; and Barnes 400-grain Buster with 62.0 grains IMR-4198 at 2,018 fps. Starline cases and Federal 210M primers were used in all loads.

Recoil? Yes, there is some. For my Marlin 1895 in .45-70 I load 300- and 400-grain bullets to respective velocities of 2,100 fps and 1,900 fps and as is to be expected, recoil feels about the same as with those bullet weights loaded to the same velocities in the .50 B&M Alaskan. Push a 500-grain bullet to 1,800 fps in the .50, and while you know you are not shooting a .45-70, the recoil will likely go unnoticed on a rainy Alaska day with a big grizzly at 30 paces and closing fast.

Since the Browning was a bit heavier I figured it would be more comfortable to shoot, but the Marlin won out. The difference was not great, but it was there.

McCourry says the Marlin Guide Gun is not a good candidate for the conversion because excessive drop in its straight-grip stock makes it less comfortable to shoot than Model 1895 variations with curved grips. I'm thinking the Model 1895XLR with its stainless steel barreled action and laminated wood stock is the ideal candidate for the conversion.

Both of the carbines I shot were very nice, and either would be just the thing for a bear guide or for the fisherman who needs protection in bear country. For my own use I would prefer a 22-inch barrel. A bit more barrel out front would dampen muzzle climb a bit and also put muzzle blast farther from the ears. I'm thinking the longer tube would increase velocity by 75 to 100 fps. I cannot think of anything else I would change about either rifle.

CREED-MORE!

O'Connor had his .270. *RifleShooter's* editor has his own favorite.

By J. Scott Rupp

Me and Jack O'Connor are a lot alike. He was one of the greatest sheep hunters of all time, with four Grand Slams. I also killed a sheep once. He hunted all over Africa and took the Big Five. I've killed two Cape buffalo and a handful of plains game. He was the most famous and prolific gun writer of all time, with countless magazine articles and several books to his credit. I have also written several articles on guns.

So you see, me and Jack are like two peas in a pod. But here's where we part company. He was a champion of the .270 Winchester. I am fast becoming a champion of the 6.5 Creedmoor. Now, granted, there are a lot of people who would be more impressed if someone of Jack's status was leading the charge for the Creedmoor, but as editor in chief of *RifleShooter*, my opinion counts too—mostly because there's no one to stop me from publishing it.

It seems like ages ago, but it was only 2008 when Hornady invited me to its Grand Island, Nebraska, plant to get the lowdown on a new competition cartridge that engineers Joe Thielen and Dave Emary had developed: the 6.5 Creedmoor. We'd just about wrapped up the interviews when none other than Steve Hornady walked into the conference room. "So what do you think?" he asked.

What do I think? You mean with several of the best and brightest people in the ammo biz looking at me, expecting some kind of intelligent observation? I tried hard to think of something intelligent, but all I could blurt out was, "Are you going to make this into a hunting round?"

Covert glances passed around the table. "Well . . ." Steve said, launching into a spiel about how they certainly could but that wasn't their intention and they really just wanted to build a great competition cartridge. But I knew I had them. A year or so later, Hornady added SST and GMX hunting bullets to the 6.5 Creedmoor lineup.

Now here's where a writer would normally insert the phrase, ". . . and the rest is history." Maybe it is, maybe it isn't. After all, the .260 Remington failed to catch on. But I do think we may be looking at one of the most versatile hunting rounds to come down the pike since the .260.

The 6.5's main claim to fame as a caliber is its incredible

sectional density and typically excellent ballistic coefficient. Take a look at the accompanying chart that compares various factory bullets loaded by Hornady (used because Hornady is the only outfit currently loading the Creedmoor). Quibble with this comparison if you will, but I think it's valid.

Of the bullets listed here, only the 180-grain .30 caliber has a better SD. Could you find heavy-for-caliber examples that would top the 6.5? Sure. The 150-grain 7mm for one, which has an SD of .266 (or the 160-grain 7mm with an exceptional SD of .283). But in order to do fair ballistics comparisons I limited bullet weight selection to those available in Hornady's non-magnum chamberings.

While it's only one element that governs terminal performance, sectional density is an important one. SD is the ratio of a bullet's mass to its cross-section, and bullets with high SDs penetrate better than those with low SDs, all other factors being equal. And penetration, of course, is key to clean kills.

Note, too, that the 6.5's BCs are chart-toppers. These high coefficients mean the bullets move well through the air, which helps them maintain velocity and reduces drop and wind drift. Less drop and drift translate to a little more margin of error if you misjudge the distance, shot angle or wind speed and direction. And more impact velocity certainly doesn't hurt.

The 6.5 Creedmoor is built on the .30 TC case, capitalizing on the short, efficient cartridge principle. As mentioned, it's currently

available in a 129-grain SST and a 120-grain GMX, both Superformance loads. The accompanying chart compares these loads with other cartridges Hornady loads with its Superformance powder—the only way I could make it an apples-to-apples comparison because Superformance loads are faster than standard loads.

Observations? All but the .243 are still carrying the generally

accepted 1,000 ft.-lbs. of energy necessary to kill a deer out to 500 yards, which I grant you is farther than we have any business shooting at deer-size game in the first place. At the far more practical distance of 300 yards, which is still a very long shot, every cartridge on that list will kill a deer, antelope or sheep without a problem.

From here we start splitting hairs. Jack O'Connor's .270 with a 130-grain bullet is the flattest of the bunch, and with a 140-grain bullet it drifts less in the wind than any of the others. But the

My first hunting experience with the Creedmoor came at Tejon Ranch in California. The Hornady guys loaded up some GMX ammo for a hog hunt. It was my first experience not just with the Creedmoor but also the GMX, a non-lead bullet (which we have to use in my part of California; for more on this, see Craig Boddington's feature elsewhere in this issue).

The 6.5 Creedmoor has excellent ballistics, but what makes it really shine is you get that performance with little recoil. And for most of us, that means you'll shoot it better.

129-grain SST Creedmoor is right there—delivering a bullet with better sectional density and with a third less recoil.

That, in a nutshell, is why I like the Creedmoor so much: eminently respectable ballistic performance with little recoil. These same characteristics have made me a believer in cartridges such as the .25-06 and 7mm-08. The Creedmoor will do anything those two will do, in some cases do it better, and in all cases do it with less recoil. That's win-win in my book.

SUPERFORMANCE BALLISTICS COMPARISON

Cartridge	Bullet Weight (gr.)	Muzzle Velocity	Muzzle Energy	Recoil Energy	100 YARDS		300 YARDS				500 YARDS			
					Velocity	Energy	Velocity	Energy	Drop	Drift	Velocity	Energy	Drop	Drift
.243 Win.	95	3,185	2,139	11.1	2,908	1,784	2,402	1,217	-6.3	7.5	1,950	802	-38.4	23.0
.25-06 Rem.	117	3,110	2,512	16.5	2,861	2,127	2,403	1,500	-6.4	6.9	1,989	1,028	-38.6	21.2
6.5 Creed.	120*	3,010	2,414	13.9	2,807	2,099	2,427	1,569	-6.5	6.2	2,078	1,150	-38.3	18.7
6.5 Creed	129	2,950	2,493	14.8	2,757	2,176	2,393	1,641	-6.8	5.8	2,059	1,214	-39.5	17.6
.270 Win.	130	3,200	2,955	19.8	2,984	2,570	2,582	1,924	-5.7	5.5	2,213	1,414	-33.7	16.6
.270 Win.	140	3,090	2,968	20.9	2,894	2,603	2,526	1,983	-6.1	5.3	2,187	1,487	-35.4	16.0
7mm-08 Rem.	139	2,950	2,686	16.5	2,757	2,345	2,393	1,768	-6.8	5.8	2,059	1,308	-39.6	17.5
.280 Rem.	139	3,090	2,946	20.7	2,890	2,578	2,516	1,954	-6.1	5.4	2,172	1,456	-35.7	16.3
.308 Win.	150	3,000	2,997	19.1	2,772	2,558	2,348	1,836	-6.9	6.8	1,963	1,282	-40.7	20.7
.30-06	165	2,960	3,209	24.2	2,750	2,769	2,357	2,034	-7.0	6.3	1,997	1,461	-40.7	19.3
.30-06	180	2,820	3,179	25.3	2,640	2,764	2,272	2,063	-7.6	6.3	1,994	1,509	-44.1	19.1

Notes: Except as noted, all cartridges are loaded with SST bullets (* GMX). Recoil energy figures were calculated with 7 lb. rifle weight and a powder velocity of 4,000 fps. Bullet velocities in feet per second. Bullet energy and recoil energy figures are in foot-pounds. Drop and drift are in inches and are not included in 100-yard figures.

Late on the first day, we got on a herd of pigs, and guide Cody Plank tried to direct me to a big hog behind a screen of trees. After much back and forth, I had the pig in my sights—offhand at about 80 yards, with a narrow window to shoot through. I shouldered the Ruger Model 77 Hawkeye, peered through the Trijicon AccuPoint and broke the shot. The pig simply dropped and rolled down the hill.

And then about a year later, "she" walked into my life. I got invited to the Yamaha Single Shot Challenge, a mule deer hunt in New Mexico with one of my favorite outfitters, Steve Jones (backcountryhunts.com). We could bring any rifle we wanted. Ruger had just announced it was chambering the No. 1 in 6.5 Creedmoor, and it took me all of two seconds to call Ruger and borrow one for the trip.

I've always had a thing for the No. 1, and by this time I was really taken with the Creedmoor due to the time I had spent with the Model 77 in the field and on the range. And the No. 1 shot like a dream. It didn't like the GMX too much, but it simply adored the 129-grain SST, drilling nice little 1/2- to 3/4-inch groups all day long, topped with the same Trijicon AccuPoint I'd had on the Model 77.

I dialed in the scope to be dead on at 200. At 300 yards I could ring the steel target at my home range by holding just a touch high of center, and on the 400-yard ram I could simply center the bottom post of the duplex, where it narrows, and pull the trigger. Ping.

Single Shot Challenge? Bring it on.

The first day, guide Donn "Deadeye" Allen and I bombed around in a decked-out Yamaha side-by-side ATV, looking for deer. I also hiked along a dry creek bed to try to move some deer for other hunters, and that gave Donn the idea to go back and hunt the creek bed the next day.

His instincts were spot on. The next morning we spooked a good buck out of the thick brush lining the creek bed. As the mulie ran uphill, I set up my shooting sticks and got behind the rifle.

The 4x4 buck was 320 yards away when I launched the first round. Miss, low. So much for the meeting the Single Shot Challenge. I shot again when he was 350 yards out. Under again, and I realized I was compensating too much for the uphill angle.

The buck stopped one more time, at just a shade under 400,

The 6.5 Creedmoor (l.) and 7mm-08 are similar performers. The 7-08 has the edge in energy due to its heavier bullet, but the 6.5's lighter bullet has better sectional density, and the round recoils less.

BULLET COMPARISON

Caliber	Weight (gr.)	BC	SD
.243	95	.355	.230
.25	117	.390	.253
6.5mm	120	.450	.246
6.5mm	129	.485	.264
.270	130	.460	.242
.270	140	.495	.261
7mm	139	.486	.246
.30	150	.415	.226
.30	165	.447	.248
.30	180	.480	.271

For comparison, all are Hornady factory-loaded GMX or SST (which have identical BCs and SDs).

of elevation clicks on the Trijicon and gave it a whirl. The first shot went way high (I was never good at math), the second still too high, but I rang it on the third.

Now I'm not the greatest shot in the world by any means, but previous shooters—with their .308s, their .300s, their 7 Rem Mags—had taken a fair number of shots to hit that target. With the flat-shooting, accurate 6.5, I did it in three. It was all the rifle and cartridge, but of course I took the credit and retired to the cook tent for a celebratory beer.

As of this writing, Ruger plans to continue offering both the 77 Hawkeye and the No. 1 in 6.5 Creedmoor. Savage Arms chambers it in the Model 16 Weather Warrior and the Model 12 LRP. Thompson/Center is also chambering the Creedmoor in the excellent Icon.

So where does that leave us? As the proud owner of the No. 1 I used in New Mexico—the check for which I wrote the day I got back from that trip—I would like to predict a great future for it.

But things are very different today than they were back in the days when Jack O'Connor sung the praises of the .270. Back then, hunters weren't so specialized, information wasn't so fast-paced and widely available, and there weren't so many damn choices.

For the Creedmoor to flourish, ammo makers such as Federal, Winchester and Remington are going to have to decide the cartridge has legs, and of course for that to happen more gun makers are going to have to see the light as well. The three that are on board represent a great start, but it will take more for the Creedmoor to make the jump from niche round to widely accepted one.

And the fine hunters and shooters out there who read this are going to have to decide that the Creedmoor is the real deal, something they want. I think Jack O'Connor would've liked it. I know I do.

where the 6.5 Creedmoor is still running at 2,222 fps and carrying 1,414 ft.-lbs. of energy. I took the same hold I'd used on the 400-yard steel ram at home, and this time when the rifle barked, the buck toppled. The bullet punched low through the chest, showing excellent expansion on the exit wound.

On the last day of the trip, we set up a steel ram on a ridge across from camp, and with the light fading (and with a couple of Surefire flashlights strategically jury-rigged to illuminate the ram) we took turns trying to smack steel at a ranged 840 yards. When my turn came, I grabbed the No. 1, ran a bunch

A FAMILY AFFAIR

THE .308 WIN. AND ITS OFFSPRING ARE POPULAR FAVORITES FOR ACCURACY- AND PERFORMANCE-MINDED SHOOTERS.

by Layne Simpson

The .308 Win. is an incredibly versatile cartridge in its own right, capable of taking game as large as red stag out to reasonable distances.

Regardless of what products a company develops or invents, there are bound to be a few losers in the mix. Chevrolet had the Corvair, Remington had the EtronX, and Winchester's underachievers include the .225 Win. and the .25 WSSM. Conversely, companies come up with some real winners as well. Winchester has had its share of those, and the .308 Win. is one of the more successful examples.

The .308 story begins shortly after the final shots of World War I had been fired. The development of ball powders by Winchester prompted a search by the U.S. Ordnance Corps for a cartridge more compact than the .30-06 but similar in performance. For a while the .300 Savage was a strong contender, and several experimental rifles were chambered for it. But its case neck proved to be a bit short for preventing bullet slippage under battlefield conditions. So the neck was lengthened by increasing case length another 0.44 inch. And changing the shoulder angle from 30 degrees to 20 degrees made the case easier to form on high-production machinery. The result was a new case with a two-grain increase in water capacity over the .300 Savage.

After about 35 years of development at Frankford Arsenal, the 7.62x51 NATO was finally adopted by the U.S. Army in 1953. It made its first military appearance in 1960 in a modified version of the M1 Garand called the M14 and in the M50 machine gun.

Winchester had been involved in the development of the cartridge since day one, and that, along with blessings from the U.S. government, enabled the company to introduce it to the commercial market as the .308 Win. a couple of years prior to its official military adoption. The cartridge made its debut in the Model 70 rifle, and though it was almost ignored to death by hunters and shooters early on, the stubby cartridge eventually caught on big time. Regardless of whether a popularity chart is based on the annual sales of ammunition or loading dies, the .308 has long ranked among the top five big game cartridges.

While they were developing the 7.62/.308, the technicians at Winchester looked closely at cartridges of other calibers on the same case. The cartridge that became the .243 Win. is almost a spitting image of Warren Page's earlier 6mm Super Pooper, but the genesis of the commercial round came about when word of Remington's upcoming .244 cartridge leaked out. The guys at Winchester quickly necked down the .308 case for bullets of the same .243-inch diameter and introduced it as the .243 Win. in 1955, the same year the .244 was unveiled by Remington.

Loaded with a 100-grain bullet for deer, the .243 took off like scalded dog and has yet to slow down. The .244 leaped from the starting gate and fell flat on the nose of its lighter 90-grain bullet. Based on both reloading die and ammunition sales for rifle cartridges above .224 caliber, the .243 Win. has remained among the top five most popular for the past 54 years.

There are several .243s in our family, but two have accounted for the most game through the years. One, a pre-'64 Winchester Model 70 Featherweight, belongs to my wife, Phyllis. Among her accomplishments with that rifle is a pronghorn antelope so good it took me quite a few years to catch up. My favorite .243 is a Model 15 Ti built around a titanium action by Prairie Gun Works, the Canadian firm. It pegs the scale at 6.5 pounds with scope and is the only rifle of its

(From l.) The U.S. military wanted a cartridge to replace the .30-06, and while the .300 Savage did get a cursory look, ultimately the round that commercially became the .308 won the race. It spawned a number of excellent short-action cartridges: .243 Win., .260 Rem., 7mm-08 Rem., .338 Federal, and .358 Win.

.308
ALSO-RANS

Many of the .308 offspring started life as wildcats. One member of the .308 family that never advanced beyond the wildcat stage was the .22-243 Middlestead. Developed and written about during the 1960s by Paul Middlestead, it was created by necking down the .243 Win. case. It generates about 200 fps higher velocities than the .220 Swift when both are loaded with bullets weighing 60 grains and heavier.

Not much is heard from the cartridge these days, but in a 26- or 28-inch barrel with a rifling twist rate of 1:9 or perhaps a bit quicker, it might be fun to load with some of today's extremely long-for-caliber bullets. The .22-243 loaded with the 53-grain Barnes TSX, 60-grain Nosler Partition or 75-grain Swift Scirocco II might be just the ticket for those who use .22 centerfires on deer.

No one seems to know who necked down the .308 case (or necked up the .243 case) and called it the .25 Souper. Few are even aware of it today. Why Winchester never got around to adopting it will never be known, but my guess is it's because it offers no improvement in performance over the .257 Roberts, which has been around since 1934. On second thought, since the .243 Win. won out over the .244 Rem. back in the 1950s, a .257 Win. might have eventually become more popular than the .257 Remington-Roberts (as it was originally called).

Reloading dies for the .22-243 Middlestead and .25 Souper are available from Redding and RCBS. Clymer and JGS Precision have the chamber reamers and headspace gauges.—LS

weight I have owned that consistently shoots three bullets inside a half-minute of angle.

The second .308 offspring was made by necking its case up for .358-inch bullets. In a world of scope-sighted rifles, the grand old Model 71 lever action was growing more obsolete each year and the flat-nosed bullet of its cartridge, the .348 Win., had become old hat. Seeing the handwriting on the wall, Winchester's engineers began designing the Model 71's replacement in 1952 and introduced it in 1955 as the Model 88. During the Model 88's first year of production, it was available only in .308, but the .358 Win. and .243 Win. were added in 1956. The Model 88 and the Model 70 were the only two Winchesters ever chambered for the .358.

Despite the fact that the .358 has always been the Rodney Dangerfield of the .308 family, I like it a lot—perhaps because I almost always pull for the underdog. More likely it's due to a lasting fondness for my Winchester 88 in this caliber. All things considered, the .338 Federal is probably a better cartridge, but the way I see it, if a move is to be made to a caliber larger than .308, stopping short of .358 makes little sense.

Even with that said, I have a high opinion of the .338 Federal. Back in 1972, Roy Smith experienced an unpleasant encounter with a grizzly while carrying his Winchester 88 in .308 Win., so he rebarreled his rifle for a wildcat made by necking up the .308 case for .338-inch bullets. Several decades later Federal took up the short-action .338 flag.

I first used the .338 Federal on a Colorado elk hunt a few months prior to its introduction in 2006. At the time no factory rifle was chambered for it, so the guys at Federal sent a couple of Sako rifles in .308 Win. to Hart Rifle Barrels for rebarreling. Two loads arrived from Federal, and because the one with the Barnes 185-grain TSX was more accurate, I chose it for the hunt. One shot dropped a bull farther away than I should have been shooting.

The .338 Federal is a great little cartridge, one with performance far exceeding what its appearance might indicate. Even so, its future appears no brighter than that of the .358.

Winchester hit two big home runs when it introduced the .243 and .308, but it dropped the ball by not necking the same case down to 7mm—which metallic silhouette competitors had done long before such a round became a factory cartridge. When it did finally reach factory status, the boxes were green and not red.

Remington introduced the 7mm-08 in the Model 788 rifle in 1980, and it went on to become the second most popular .308 offspring.

I still have one of the first 788s made during that year, and it is the most accurate factory rifle in 7mm-08 I have ever shot. The very first Model Seven FS carbine built by the Remington custom shop also resides in my gun room, and since it weighs only 6.25 pounds with scope, it is better for toting up steep mountains. Through the years I have taken quite a bit of game with the little rifle, but my favorite and most accurate 7mm-08 was built by Kenny Jarrett some years back around a Model Seven action.

Little guys sometimes get trampled in a new cartridge introduction stampede, and the .260 Rem. story begins with just that. Around 1996, Art Alphin of A-Square submitted

The .243 Win., here in a pre-'64 Model 70, is one of the most popular deer cartridges of all time and one that remains a favorite even after 54 years of existence.

The 7mm-08, here in a Remington Seven FS, was first a wildcat popular among silhouette shooters. Today it's also known as a capable hunting cartridge and a solid seller.

SELECTED .308 FAMILY LOADS

BULLET	Bullet Weight (gr.)	Powder Type	Powder Charge (gr.)	Muzzle Velocity (fps)	Standard Deviation	Avg. Group (in.)
.243 WIN. (1)						
SIERRA BLITZKING	70	Hodgdon Varget	40.0	3,419	28	0.74
NOSLER PARTITION	85	Hodgdon H4831SC	44.0	3,064	19	1.25
.260 REM. (2)						
HORNADY GMX	120	Hodgdon H4831SC	45.0	2,862	28	1.15
HORNADY SST	129	Vihtavuori N165	49.0	2,884	18	1.38
7MM-08 REM. (3)						
HORNADY V-MAX	120	Alliant Reloder 15	43.0	2,902	15	0.32
HORNADY SST	139	Ramshot Big Game	48.0	2,751	19	0.40
.308 WIN. (4)						
NOSLER BALLISTIC TIP	125	Winchester 760	52.0	3,029	18	0.29
NOSLER PARTITION	165	Hodgdon Varget	46.0	2,760	29	0.33
.338 FEDERAL (5)						
BARNES TSXBT	185	Accurate 2230	40.0	2,703	26	1.28
NOSLER PARTITION	210	Alliant Reloder 15	46.0	2,472	10	1.33
.358 WIN. (6)						
BARNES TSXBT	200	Hodgdon Benchmark	46.0	2,466	14	1.45
SWIFT A-FRAME	225	IMR 4895	48.0	2,410	17	1.52

NOTES: Accuracy results are for five three-shot groups from a benchrest at 100 yards. Velocities are averages of 15 rounds clocked 12 feet from the muzzle by an Oehler Model 33 chronograph. Hornady cases were used (.260 Remington and .338 Federal were formed from .308 cases). CCI 200 primers were used in all loads. Rifle Legend: (1) Pre-'64 Win. 70 Featherweight, 22 in. barrel; (2) Remington Seven CDL, 22 in. barrel; (3) Jarrett Rem. Seven, 22 in. barrel; (4) Jarrett Rem. Seven, 21 in. barrel; (5) Sako 75, 22 in. barrel; (6) Winchester 88, 22 in. barrel

paperwork on the 6.5-08 A-Square— a .308 necked down to 6.5, as the designation suggests— to SAAMI. A bit later, Remington submitted the .260 Rem., a cartridge on the 7mm-08 Rem. case, which is .020 inch longer than the .308 case. Today there is no 6.5-308 A-Square (nor a .260 Panther, which is what one version of the .260 was also called). Remington obviously won the match.

The .260 Rem. and I got off to a really bad start. The first rifle I shot it in, a Model 700 Titanium Ultimate Lightweight, still holds the record as being the most inaccurate Model 700 I have ever rested atop sandbags. Checking the rifling twist rate of its barrel did not dawn on me, but as I now understand, early rifles had the same 1:10 twist that had worked nicely with rifles in 6.5 Rem. Mag.

But the .260 is slower, so the twist rate was increased to 1:8. I later shot the .260 in a couple of other rifles with the quicker twist and had no complaint with their accuracy.

I eventually had a heavy, match-grade barrel in .260 Rem. installed on my switch-barrel Model 700 target rifle. It is quite accurate, but average group size has never quite equaled those fired by the same rifle with barrels of the same make in 6.5-284 Norma and 6.5 Creedmoor. But that's likely nothing more than luck of the draw as a good rifle in .260 Rem. should be able to shoot along with the best of them. I have bumped off three deer, one black bear and several hogs with rifles chambered for this cartridge, and while that does not make me an expert on its capabilities, it seemed to

kill all as dead as is possible with any other member of the .308 family.

All things considered from a big game hunter's point of view, the .308 Win. is probably the best all-around choice of the entire clan. When loaded to 3,000 fps or so with the Nosler 125-grain Ballistic Tip, it will hold its own with either of its offspring in pronghorn country. Load it to maximum speed with a good 150-grain bullet and it becomes a darned good deer cartridge. Move up in bullet weight to 165 or 180 grains and it is not a bad elk cartridge at reasonable distances. Owning one rifle in .308 would cover most of the hunting most of us do, but as I long discovered, having rifles chambered for the entire family is a lot more fun.

THE
VERSATILITY KING

by Craig Boddington _____

Describing the .375 H&H as one of the world's most versatile cartridges is correct, especially if you're thinking on a global scale. Although more powerful than needed for most North American game, it actually shoots flat enough for most hunting conditions, and with the proper bullets it has the power and penetration needed to handle the world's largest game.

Looked at another way, it's actually a "jack of all trades and master of none." Throughout the world the list of game for which it is actually ideally suited is fairly short. However, there is no African jurisdiction where the .375 H&H is not legal all the way up to elephant, and in some countries it is the stated minimum for "thick-skinned dangerous game." So despite all arguments, whether theoretical or practical, the .375 is the minimum choice to hunt the entire world's game.

Let's emphasize that word "minimum." Despite the untold numbers of buffalo cleanly taken with the cartridge, I'm certain the .40s and .416s are better for the big bovines, and calibers larger than .40 are much better for elephant. However, the combination of lower velocity, arcing trajectory and heavy recoil render these more powerful cartridges less versatile. The .375 will get the job done on the big stuff—and, if required, it can reach out quite a ways on the smaller stuff. It actually can do it all, and with that capability it stands almost alone (along with some of its .375-diameter stablemates, of course).

I was a late teenager when I got my first .375 H&H. A child of the first magnum craze, I was more enamored of raw power (and more resistant to recoil) than I am today. I used that old .375 to take my first elk, my first moose, my first wild sheep, my first caribou and my first grizzly, and it accounted for several deer and a couple of pronghorns as well.

It might not have been the best choice in some applications, but it got the job done. Since then I've done a bit of elk and bear hunting with the .375, but no more sheep. However, I have never gotten over my love affair with the caliber, and I have always had at least one .375 H&H.

In preparation for this article, I dug through the gun safes and discovered—with some amusement—that I had on hand five .375 H&Hs and two .375 Rugers. Some are test guns, but clearly I like the caliber. Over here I haven't chosen the .375 for deer-size game for nearly 40 years, but in Africa, where you don't know what you might encounter on a given day, I've used various .375s to take a tremendous variety of plains game small and large, and of course I've used it for the big stuff as well.

Often it has been the heavier of a two-rifle battery, but sometimes the lighter, mated with a true big-bore. On several occasions it has provided excellent service as a one-rifle safari battery. In fact, a .375 remains the only caliber I would choose for a one-rifle safari that includes both dangerous and non-dangerous game.

It really can do it all. In 1981, I used it to take an Alaskan brown bear that I will never see the equal of. In Zambia in 1984, I killed a huge Kafue lechwe at perhaps 450 yards (in pre-rangefinder days). In South Africa in 2006, we had a running gun battle going with a wounded leopard, and I stopped it with a station 8 skeet shot when the leopard went airborne. In Cameroon in 2008, I shot what I consider my best African trophy, a monstrous Derby eland—taken with a single 270-grain Hornady Interlock across 250 yards of dead-flat burned ground.

Over the years I've learned a lot about the H&H cartridge and caliber overall. I learned a bit more while spending some quality range time for this article. Here are some observations.

First off, I have never encountered any "bad" .375 bullets. In this regard it's a lot like the .30-06. Excepting the light bullets intended for the .375 Win., all .375 bullets are designed to perform well at .375 H&H velocities. With 101 years of development, they perform nicely, and they should. The moderate velocity probably contributes to good performance. With the very fast .375s you might need to be a bit more careful about bullet selection, but at classic .375 H&H velocities, great bullet performance can be expected.

Holland & Holland brought out the .375 H&H Mag. in 1912, initially with three loads: a fast, light-for-caliber, 235-grain bullet; a 270-grain

bullet at credible velocity; and a workhorse 300-grain bullet in both expanding and solid form. The 235-grain bullet fell by the wayside (probably because it was used on game it wasn't designed for), and today 270- and 300-grain bullets remain the standard choices. There are others, and some are useful, but these remain the most popular and most common choices.

The 270-grain bullet is standard at 2,690 fps. Ballistically it compares well with a 180-grain bullet from a .30-06, which is standard at 2,700, and has a similar sectional density: .271 for the 180-grain .30 caliber, .274 for the 270-grain .375. The .375 bullet generally has an inferior ballistic coefficient compared to a .30 caliber bullet, but at normal hunting ranges the trajectory is similar and thus familiar. With most 270-grain loads, sight in two inches high at 100 yards and you will drop nine to 10 inches at 300 yards.

The 300-grain bullet is standard at about 2,530 fps. Sectional density is better at .305, but most BCs are inferior because the majority of 300-grain bullets are roundnose, while the majority of 270-grain bullets are at least semi-spitzer.

But it depends on what you want to do with the cartridge. Nosler's 300-grain Partition is a semi-spitzer with a respectable BC of .398. Hornady's 300-grain boattail spitzer has an off-the-chart BC of .460. Other great 300-grain bullets such as the Swift A-Frame, Sierra GameKing and Federal's Trophy Bonded Bear Claw are also sharp-pointed bullets. Sight them in 2.5 inches high at 100 yards, and despite the lower initial velocity you are dead-on at 200 yards and about the same 10 inches low at 300 yards because of better aerodynamics.

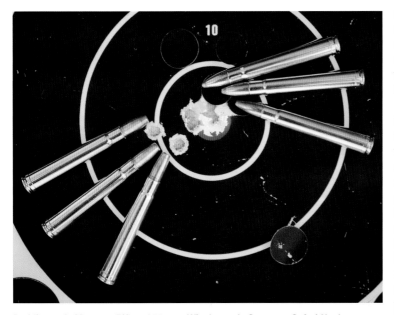

Boddington's Montana Rifles .375 puts Winchester's Supreme Safari Nosler Partitions and Nosler solids into the same spot. This is a trait of the .375, although not all rifles or loads will do it.

The .375's versatility really shines in Africa, where it can be either the "big" or "little" component of a two-gun battery—and also a great candidate as a single rifle to take when dangerous and non-dangerous game are on the menu.

When I started using the .375, Africa was only a dream. I used mostly the faster 270-grain bullets. They worked well, but eventually I figured out the ballistics facts, and for most of my life I have been a staunch 300-grain guy. Aside from more weight, which only matters on large game, a primary advantage to the 300-grain expanding bullet is that it's the same weight as the standard 300-grain solid, which means both styles will shoot close to the same point of impact. That's important on African dangerous game, where you typically start with an expanding bullet and then use solids for follow-ups.

The .375 is legendary for printing various loads and bullet weights in the same group. It is a forgiving cartridge, and if you stick with the same bullet weights this is reasonably true—at least within the level of accuracy needed for a 300-grain solid. But don't count on it. As with any cartridge, significant shifts can occur from one bullet to another, and when you change bullet weights the shifts can be dramatic. You have to check.

For many years, the 300-grain Sierra GameKing was one of my favorite .375 bullets. Back when published loads were less conservative, my preferred handload was a slightly compressed case full of IMR 4350. In a 25-inch barrel I got an honest 2,600 fps. That flattens things out very well.

Nobody has hunted with all the great .375 bullets, but I've also had wonderful results with numerous other 300-grain expanding bullets: Swift A-Frame, Nosler Partition, Hornady DGX, Woodleigh Weld Core, Trophy Bonded Bear Claw, Barnes TSX. They're all good.

A Little Less Kick

That said, I started with the old semi-spitzer 270-grain Remington Core-Lokt, and in the last few years I've gone back to 270-grain bullets quite a bit. They don't necessarily shoot flatter, but they do kick a bit less. The one I've used the most in recent years is Hornady's 270-grain Spire Point InterLock, and I've seen a fair number of other 270-grain .375 bullets in use on game up to buffalo, and with modern bullets I haven't seen much difference in effect or performance between that weight and 300-grain bullets.

While the standard velocities for the 270- and 300-grain bullets are

If there's one pursuit the .375 H&H is perfect for, it's North America's big bears. The round's flat trajectory and power, coupled with relatively mild recoil, make it a terrific choice. This bruin fell to 300-grain Sierra GameKings.

2,690 and 2,530 fps, respectively, for some reason .375 H&H velocities are all over the map. A couple of days ago I chronographed 13 different 300-grain factory loads in guns with barrels of 22, 23, 24 and 25 inches. Obviously the 25-inch barrel produced the highest velocity; the loss for the 24-inch length was negligible and even at 22 inches was not significant. What was significant was that, among those 13 loads, velocities varied by a dramatic 200 fps—from a low of just over 2,400 fps to a sizzling high of 2,600 fps.

Of all the loads I chronographed, only Hornady 300-grain DGX and DGS, Nosler Safari 300-grain Partition and Solid and Remington 300-grain Swift A-Frame actually came up to the traditional 2,530 fps—and in a 25-inch barreled CZ550 these loads all delivered a bonus.

All other 300-grain loads were slower. In most cases the loss was an insignificant 40 or 50 fps, which no buffalo will ever notice, but if you're relying on your .375 for its great versatility, this will throw off your ballistics chart. I have rarely encountered such a spread. It suggests that, as always, you should select your load based on accuracy and desired bullet performance—and then chronograph it so you know exactly what you're dealing with.

The .375 H&H is an accurate cartridge. It is not as much fun to shoot groups with a .375 as with a .222 Rem., but it shoots well. Most big bores do because slight variations in bullets and bores are not as significant as in smaller diameters. However, optimum accuracy is made more difficult by recoil and the fact that we tend to put low-powered scopes on our .375s. Even so, I expect a .375 to shoot, and I don't remember ever seeing one that wouldn't.

Over the years I've seen the occasional quarter-inch group, which is probably a fluke with a 4X or 5X scope. I've seen a lot more groups from 0.5 to 0.75 m.o.a., and I don't think I've ever seen a .375 that wouldn't group 1.5 m.o.a. with some loads. Nobody ever said the .375 was a long-range cartridge, so the accuracy is plenty good enough for the cartridge's purposes.

There are ways to expand .375 H&H performance. You can go down in bullet weight and increase velocity for lighter game, or you can go up in bullet weight and increase penetration on larger game. For me the former path is the most interesting. Although the original 235-grain Kynoch load didn't go the distance, for decades Speer has offered a 235-grain semi-spitzer. Jack Carter had an original Bear Blaw in 240 grains, and Barnes makes a 235-grain TSX.

You can push these bullets fast. Even with today's conservative reloading manuals, 2,900 fps is attainable, and 3,000 fps might be possible. When I was a kid, I shot jackrabbits and prairie dogs with the 235-grain Speer, and I also used it on plains game up to kudu. Although SD and BC figures are low, high initial velocity wins at normal hunting ranges, so these light bullets are excellent if you want to use a .375 for elk or moose. And in spite of the velocity, recoil is mild.

Sierra also has a 250-grain GameKing boattail, and perhaps the most popular light .375 bullet is Nosler's 260-grain AccuBond. Both can be pushed to at least 2,800 fps. These light bullets actually extend the versatility of the .375 into normal North American hunting situations. Today I really can't imagine anyone choosing a .375 for deer or pronghorn, but if you have one and you want to use it, the lighter bullets offer excellent options.

I am lukewarm on the extra-heavy bullets. In factory ammo, Norma is

SELECT .375 H&H LOADS

Bullet	Bullet Weight (gr.)	Powder	Powder Charge (gr.)	Primer	Muzzle Velocity (gr.)	Source	Notes
BARNES TSX	235	Win. 748	87	Fed. 215M	3,050	Barnes	awesome elk load
SPEER SS	235	IMR 4064	77	Fed. 215M	3,000	Speer	plains game and prairie dogs
NOSLER ACCUBOND	260	RL 15	73	Rem 9.5M	2,793	Nosler	elk, moose, large plains game
HORNADY SPIRE POINT	270	IMR 4064	73.4	Win. WLRM	2,700	Hornady	large game up to buffalo
BARNES TSX	270	Vit. N540	78.5	Fed 215M	2,836	Barnes	large game up to buffalo
HORNADY*	300	IMR 4064	68.7	Win WLRM	2,500	Hornady	4064 said to be O'Connor's favorite in .375
VARIOUS**	300	IMR 4350	see note	Fed 215M	2,550	various	author's favorite load

NOTES: All loads are at or near published maximums. Reduce 5 percent and work up using responsible reloading procedures. All velocities suggested from 24-inch barrel. Actual velocities will vary. Abbreviation: SS, semi-spitzer.
* Suitable for maker's DGX, DGS and boattail spire-point bullets.
** Suitable for Sierra GameKing, Nosler Partition, Swift A-Frame. Published maximums and velocities vary among manuals. 71 grains is good starting load; work up in 1/2-grain increments. Published maximums are 75 to 77 grains; author's best results required slightly compressed loads.

WARNING: The loads shown here are safe only in the guns for which they were developed. Neither the author nor Skyhorse Publishing assumes any liability for accidents or injury resulting from the use or misuse of this data. Shooting reloads may void any warranty on your firearm.

the primary source, but there are a handful of 350-grain .375s and a couple heavier than that. On buffalo, these extra-heavies offer increased penetration and may be good choices. The primary pitfall is they're slow. On the uppermost end of the scale they offer advantages, but because the trajectory is so arcing they rob the .375 of its versatility—and the difference in point of impact is so extreme you really can't use a standard bullet weight and a 350-grain heavyweight without re-zeroing the rifle.

The impact difference between a 300-grain bullet at 2,530 fps and a 350-grain bullet 20 percent slower is about seven inches at 100 yards. Penetration is awesome, and with that much more weight energy remains high, but the 300-grain .375 has been adequate for the largest game since 1912, so I'd just as soon not give up the versatility.

So what, in the final analysis, is the .375 good for? The .375 is classic for buffalo and lion and effective on both, but it might well be overkill for a 400-pound thin-skinned lion, and the "over .40s" offer more instant gratification on buffalo. However, it is a traditional, classic and frankly perfect choice for our largest bears, which can weigh almost as much as

African buffalo but aren't as thick-skinned. It is perfect for eland, Africa's largest antelope. An eland bull is bigger than a buffalo but not as tough.

Honestly, I can't think of much else the .375 is perfect for. But that isn't its strong suit. Where it really shines is as a go-anywhere, do-anything cartridge. It hits hard, shoots flat and straight, and its bullets perform amazingly well. Choose those bullets wisely, and there isn't much you can't do with it, which is why it has remained a world standard for fully 100 years.

THE MIGHTY '06

AMERICA'S FAVORITE CENTERFIRE CARTRIDGE IS A LOT MORE CAPABLE THAN YOU MIGHT THINK.

by Craig Boddington

Jack O'Connor was arguably America's greatest gun writer. The .270 Win. was his favorite cartridge, and he championed it for 50 years. In print it was always clear that he preferred the .270, but he was kind to many other cartridges. The .30-06 was one of the cartridges he was consistently kind to. Although he never said this in print, in a letter to Ken Elliott (first editor and longtime publisher of *Petersen's Hunting*), O'Connor actually conceded that the .30-06 was more versatile than his pet .270.

Yes, indeed it is. Now seven years into its second century, the .30-06 remains not just America's favorite hunting cartridge but also a world standard. One could argue it's a bit light for the big bears, and certainly it's a poor choice (and generally illegal) for Africa's largest game. But there is very little one cannot do with a .30-06 anywhere on the planet, and there are .30 caliber bullets well-suited for any game appropriate to hunt with an '06.

In the late 1950s, Grancel Fitz became the first hunter to take all varieties of North American big game—still a feat accomplished by very few—and he did it all with his trusty Springfield in .30-06. Much more recently, my friend J. Y. Jones completed his quest for all the North American species. He did it with his battered and much-loved Remington .30-06.

Let's think about that for just a moment. One might easily imagine loading up 200- or 220-grain heavyweights for the biggest bears. But just supposing you drew the tags or won the lottery. Would you entrust the four North American sheep to a .30-06? Honestly, I would not; there are better tools for such specialized pursuits. I've hunted mountain game elsewhere in the world with a .30-06, but not in North America. I haven't used it for big bears, either.

And yet the .30-06 has been one of my favorite cartridges for more

than 35 years. As O'Connor admitted, it's a versatility king—excellent for most deer hunting, awesome for elk, perfect for the general run of African plains game. Over the years I've had flings with many cartridges, but the .30-06 is one I keep coming back to. That said, even I have probably sold it short.

The first time I used it was in 1977, in Kenya on my first African safari. Serious jitters resulted in spectacular misses at first. Fortunately, I got past that, and at the tail end my Ruger M77 in .30-06 accounted for about a dozen one-shot kills in a row. Some of those shots were easy, others were difficult, but ever since then I've had a soft spot for the .30-06.

The following year I was off active duty and trying to make a go as a freelance writer. I had this crazy idea to take the four North American deer—whitetail, blacktail, mule deer, Coues whitetail—in a single season.

I pulled it off, and it was quite the saga. I took the whitetail with a .270, but I used the same Ruger .30-06 for the other three. The .30-06 is probably not the most ideal choice for Coues deer, but the shot I drew was routine, and it got the job done. The blacktail wasn't all that far, but he was running hell for election up an opposite ridge, and I dumped him.

The mule deer was taken in northern Nevada. On the last day a big buck boiled out of a canyon bottom. As the deer started up the far side, I jumped off my horse, laid prone on a flat rimrock and when I got set the buck was level with me, now walking. We didn't have rangefinders in those days—and, less spoiled, we were probably better at judging distance. I estimated 400 yards and held a foot over his back and just in front of his nose. The bullet caught him just behind the shoulder. At the time it was the longest shot I'd ever made on a big game animal, and I still consider it one of my best.

A lot of water has passed under the bridge since then. I've been fortunate to do a lot of hunting, and I've used a lot of cartridges. The .30-06 has remained a favorite but not a consistent choice. Instead, like a lot of long-gone riflemen, I try to pick the most ideal tool for the job at hand.

But that's not always possible. A couple years ago I had three episodes of "Petersen's Hunting Adventures" television stacked pretty close together. I was obligated to use a sponsor's rifle, and these

A cartridge that's been around as long as—and has been as popular as—the .30-06 benefits from a lot of attention from ammo makers, and chances are there will be a load that will provide decent accuracy in any given rifle.

Aside from its longevity and terminal performance, the .30-06 is also loved for its relatively mild recoil, a level that almost any shooter can handle.

hunts were allocated to Savage. That was fine, but the only Savage I had on hand was a lightweight .30-06, and I didn't have time to put anything else together.

The three hunts were an eclectic mix: Columbian whitetail in Oregon, Arctic Island caribou in the Northwest Territories and elk in Montana. The Columbian whitetail is a small deer found in rugged country in western Oregon. The season is early, and it was warm, so I found it to be a glassing hunt somewhat like Coues whitetail. In other words, the conditions weren't really ideal for the .30-06 because the shots can be long, but it got the job done just fine.

The caribou hunt was out of Cambridge Bay in sub-zero cold, a challenge for both hunters and equipment. Caribou aren't all that tough, and the Arctic Island race is the smallest of all, but most caribou country is extremely open, and Arctic tundra is the most open. I've

always figured the fast 7mms to be the ideal, but the .30-06 handled that as well. It was a simple shot down a snowy ridge at 150 yards, hardly a challenge for the '06.

Ah, but the elk hunt. Several Wounded Warriors and I were hunting open sagebrush ridges north of Missoula. There were lots of elk, but I didn't take my rifle out of the case until they had departed, which left me one day.

We found a big herd feeding below a high ridge, and there was a nice bull among them. The problem was that the distance was 350 yards, and there were far too many eyes, ears and noses to get closer. I've taken several bulls with the .30-06 and have no qualms about its capabilities—but 350 yards is a long poke on an elk. I'd have been much more comfortable with a .300, 8mm or .338 magnum. But there was nothing for it but to settle down and shoot or walk away. I piled up some packs for a rest, figured the drop,

factored in the steep angle, took the shot and got the elk.

In these days of super-fast magnums we—or at least some of us, sometimes including me—tend to consider the .30-06 as "slow" and "underpowered." Although there are many faster and more powerful cartridges, neither categorization is deserved.

At its introduction in 1906, the .30-06 was very fast for the time, and with more than a century of load development and propellant improvement, it's considerably faster now. Standard loads today include a 150-grain bullet at 2,900 fps, 165-grain bullet at 2,800 fps, and 180-grain bullet at 2,700 fps. Although not flashy, these are creditable velocities that, mated with aerodynamic bullets, allow reasonably flat trajectories and effective downrange energies.

Sure, there are faster cartridges. A .30 caliber magnum might be 10 percent faster, and there are huge-cased monster .30s that are 20 percent faster. However, it's important to remember that trajectory is just a number. What I mean is that no cartridges exist that allow shooting "all the way out," especially at the distances some people are shooting today, without adjusting for the range. At some point it becomes essential to compensate for the trajectory.

With standard loads the .30-06 can be sighted so the vital zone of a deer can be hit out to nearly 300 yards without holdover. There are a few cartridges that can be sighted to accomplish this out to 400 yards, but that's about the limit. Beyond the point where holdover is required, it is essential to know the trajectory, no matter what you are shooting.

African professional hunters love to see clients show up with an '06 for a plains game hunt. The cartridge works well for pretty much anything on the menu, and almost everyone shoots it better than they do a magnum.

SELECT .30-06 FACTORY AND HANDLOADS

Load	Bullet Weight (gr.)	Muzzle Velocity/ Energy	200 Yd. Velocity/ Energy	300 Yd. Velocity/ Energy	400 Yd. Velocity/ Energy	300 Yd. Drop (in.)	400 Yd. Drop (in.)
FEDERAL HI-SHOK	150	2,910/2,820	2,340/1,825	2,080/1,445	1,840/1,130	-8.2	-24.4
HORNADY SF SST	150	3,080/3,159	2,627/2,298	2,417/1,945	2,216/1,636	-6.4	-18.9
REMINGTON CORE-LOKT	165	2,800/2,872	2,283/1,909	2,047/1,534	1,825/1,220	-8.7	-25.9
HORNADY SF SST	165	2,960/3,209	2,549/2,380	2,357/2,034	2,173/1,729	-6.9	-20.1
WINCHESTER ACCUBOND	180	2,750/3,022	2,403/2,308	2,239/2,004	2,082/1,732	-7.9	-22.8
HORNADY SF SST	180	2,820/3,178	2,447/2,393	2,272/2,063	2,104/1,769	-7.6	-21.9
IMR 4350 ACCUBOND*	150	3,000/2,997	2,574/2,170	2,376/1,890	2,186/1,558	-6.7	-19.7
IMR 4350 INTERBOND*	165	2,900/3,081	2,494/2,279	2,304/1,945	2,123/1,651	-7.2	-21.1
RELODER 22 ACCUBOND*	180	2,800/3,133	2,448/2,396	2,282/2,978	2,123/1,820	-7.6	-22.0

NOTES: *Handloads derived from Hornady (8th Edition) and Nosler (6th Edition). Velocity figures in fps; energy figures in ft.-lbs. Trajectory based on 200-yard zero. Abbreviation: SF, Superformance.

If you know the trajectory and the range, and can read the wind, then you can continue to make hits as far as your skill level allows. If you don't know the trajectory, then you're done—again, no matter what you are shooting. Over the years I've made several fairly long shots with the .30-06, and I've missed some with faster cartridges. It's just a matter of knowing the trajectory, then holding 'em and squeezing 'em.

This was brought home in spades when Ruger introduced its American bolt action at the SAAM shooting school in Texas. Our group was a dozen gun writers and Ruger personnel, all shooting American .30-06 rifles with Hornady's M1 Garand load, a load featuring a 168-grain bullet at 2,700 fps.

After zeroing and ringing steel targets at shorter ranges, we walked every single .30-06 rifle out to 700 yards, basically without hiccups. The scopes were all Zeiss but not all the same magnification. Beyond 700 yards a few rifles ran out of scope adjustment, but we got most of them clear to 1,000 yards. Mind you, few of us were experienced 1,000-yard shooters, but historically an awful lot of 1,000-yard competition has been done effectively with the .30-06.

As for power, the .30-06 is a gentle giant. Well, maybe not so gentle. Even the .30-06 isn't for everybody. For 50 years, some military recruits complained about its recoil, but during its half-century as America's military round, it was the most powerful standard cartridge employed by a major power. In battle it was legendary for both range and knock-down power.

In the field it does the same. It is not an elephant cartridge and is marginal for the biggest bears, but it's great for elk and, if anything, overpowered for anything less. Provided you know how to use it, it also has all the distance capabilities most of us have any business employing.

Over the years the 180-grain bullet has been my most consistent choice, but realistically, the hunting bullets we have today are so much better than what we had in 1978 that it is very practical to use lighter bullets, which increase velocity, flatten trajectory and reduce recoil.

This is especially true for deer-size game. There is really no reason to use a bullet heavier than 150 grains, and tougher 150-grain bullets are just fine for elk. The 165-grain bullet is a good compromise; it's faster than the 180s but 10 percent heavier than the 150s.

Due to the .30-06's longevity and popularity, its factory loads are pretty much state of the art, but with a century of load development, it remains possible to increase performance through handloading. For folks who worship at the shrine of velocity, 150-grain bullets can easily be handloaded to break the 3,000 fps barrier, and 165-grain bullets can top 2,900 fps.

Even 180-grain velocities can be somewhat enhanced. Due to the specter of product liability, maximum loads have been gradually downgraded, so many of the load recipes I used in my youth have vanished from the loading manuals. My favorite load is one of those. It is one grain over today's maximum, so my editor isn't going to let me pass it on. All I'll say is that I drive a 180-grain bullet to 2,800 fps out of a 24-inch barrel.

Want to talk versatility? Grancel Fitz took every North American species of big game with a .30-06.

But don't fret. Thanks to newer propellants, such as Hornady Superformance (available from Hodgdon), there are some published loads that will do that and even faster. And if you don't handload, well, you can just buy factory Superformance ammo: 150-grain SST at 3,080 fps, 165-grain bullet at 2,960 fps, and 180-grain bullet at 2,820 fps.

As numbers go, this is significant because 2,890 fps, a mere 70 fps difference, is the standard velocity for factory loads for the .300 H&H with 180-grain bullets. Don't start howling: I know full well that you can handload the H&H to much higher velocity.

But that isn't the point. The point is this: In its second century the .30-06 is now achieving velocities close to what, traditionally, only larger-cased magnums could offer. In other words, the .30-06 ain't slow.

It can never be as fast as the .300 Win. Mag. or the larger-cased fast .30s, but it doesn't kick as much, doesn't need as long a barrel and has a greater magazine capacity, and its cartridges are lighter and more compact.

As I've written before, we are definitely in a new era of "magnum mania." In spite of all the brave new magnums (and the old ones), I see little evidence that the .30-06 has slipped in popularity. This is not only because it works. Rather, I think it's because a great many riflemen still recognize that it offers all the capability they really need. And, as ".270 Jack" O'Connor grudgingly conceded, it remains one of our most versatile options, without breaking bank, shoulder or eardrums.

MAGNUM OPUS

by Craig Boddington

THE FAST .30 CALIBERS ARE HARD-HITTING AND VERSATILE. IS THERE A SINGLE BEST ONE?

Not being a very imaginative writer, I get a lot of story ideas from reader letters, both good and bad. Recently, I got a thoughtful letter regarding a recent story in which I wrote about a mountain hunt with my .300 Wby. Mag., admitting I was probably over-gunned but at the same time the choice giving me confidence. The gentleman courteously took me to task, suggesting that perhaps if I learned to shoot better I'd have more confidence in Professor O'Connor's standard recommendation: a .270 Win.

Well, it's my fault because I didn't explain myself. The rifle I referred to in the story was a Blaser R8, and I actually have a .270 barrel for it. What I neglected to mention was that the hunt in question was in the Caucasus Mountains of Russia, and Asian mountain hunting is a bit different. In a lot of those big mountains, the tops are arid and almost devoid of cover. You can't always get as close as you might like, and this is often complicated by the fact that, over there, you often have an inescapable retinue of well-intentioned "helpers"—more people than you really want following around, which makes it even harder to get close to your quarry. I've used fast 6.5mms and .270s over there, and once I went up the scale and carried my 8mm Remington Magnum. But, ideally, Asian mountain hunting is "fast .30" territory.

A fast .30 actually isn't a bad choice for any mountain hunting and pretty good for elk, especially in open country. And while you may not agree with me, let's pretend to agree that a super-charged .30 caliber cartridge has its uses. A few folks must feel this way because there are a bunch of them.

All are pretty darned good, but our purpose here is to winnow through them and figure if there's one that stands out as the most sensible choice. And for this discussion, I'm going to rule out non-standard cartridges. No doubt there are some fantastic .30 caliber wildcats, but with all the over-the-counter choices we have, are the wildcats really better enough to be worth the hassle? I don't think so.

Should we include proprietaries? I'm tempted. John Lazzeroni's two .30 calibers are both the fastest in their class. His full-length 7.82 (.308) Warbird may not be the fastest .30 you can load, but for sure it's the fastest you can buy. Likewise, his short 7.82 (.308) Patriot is

the fastest short magnum, although he's no longer chambering for it. I've used them both, and I like them; as specialized tools, they are excellent. There are two limitations. Clearly, there is just a single source for both ammo and brass. Not so obvious is that both cartridges are essentially based on the big .416 Rigby diameter case with full diameter rim. Few actions are generous enough to house them, so now we have a limited selection of rifles as well as single-source ammo. For this discussion I think we'll pass on them.

Having made that decision, it's now easy to rule out the .30–.378 Wby. Mag. for exactly the same reasons: great capability, but single-source ammo and limited platforms. Other proprietaries in the fast .30 class include the .300 Dakota Mag., .300 Blaser Mag. and .308 Norma Mag. With all three one can win argument points on cartridge design and efficiency, but that's not enough to override the availability problem.

And if we're drawing this sort of line, we have to exclude the .300 Rem. Short Action Ultra Mag as well. With a 2.015-inch case the RSAUM would fit into any action, including Remington's little Model Seven action. However, the round's own parent company no longer chambers it in any of its rifles, and it offers just two factory loads. Nosler also offers two, but that's it.

This still leaves us with six fast .30s from major manufacturers. Short (.308-length) magnums: .300 Ruger Compact Mag. and .300 Win. Short Mag. Standard (.30-06-length) magnums: .300 Win. Mag. Long (.375-length) magnums: .300 H&H Mag., .300 Rem. Ultra Mag, .300 Wby. Mag. That should leave us plenty to talk about.

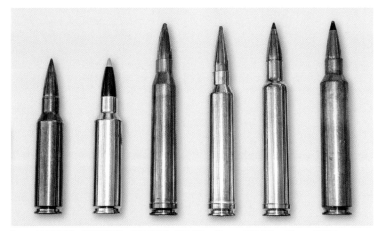

L.-r.: .300 RCM, .300 WSM, .300 H&H, .300 Win. Mag., .300 Wby. Mag., .300 Rem. Ultra Mag. These six factory cartridges represent the most available fast .30s. While Boddington believes the H&H is a bit too slow for him, there's really not a bad choice to be made.

While for years he favored the .300 Wby., Boddington is spending more time with the .300 Win. Mag., courtesy of Legendary Arms Works (top) and Kenny Jarrett (bottom) rifles. The cartridge offers good performance and unmatched availability for rifles and ammo.

SHORT MAGNUMS

Both of the short fast .30s—.300 RCM and .300 WSM—trade on the efficiency of the short, fat case to produce performance similar to the .300 Win. Mag., at least to a point. While it appears silly for two such cartridges to exist, there are subtle differences. The RCM and WSM have 2.1-inch cases and will fit into most short actions. The WSM has an "extra wide" .555-inch case with a rebated rim. The RCM is actually a clever little cartridge with a .532-inch rim and base diameter, which is the same as the rim and belt on .375 H&H-based cartridges.

Both short magnums have the capability to be housed in shorter, lighter actions, and the efficiency of their short, fat cases also tends to allow full velocity from slightly shorter barrels. So what's not to like? Well, nothing insurmountable, but there are three issues worthy of comment.

First is availability. By far the more popular is the WSM. It was first (2001) and has caught on the best. It is loaded by Black Hills, Federal, Nosler and Winchester, and

a fair number of manufacturers offer rifles chambered for it (and, perhaps telling, while Remington no longer chambers its own .300 short magnum, it does chamber the .300 WSM).

The .300 RCM is far less available, with only Hornady loading ammo and only Ruger chambering rifles for it.

Second is feeding. This is an issue inherent with the short, fat cartridges simply because few bolt actions were designed to house cartridges shaped like that. Some rifles feed better than others, some need work on the follower or rails, and a few are just plain unreliable, but it's pretty rare to find a short magnum rifle that is really smooth. The Ruger Compact Magnum with its slightly narrower case was actually designed not for maximum performance but for smoother feeding and ease of manufacture.

As far as performance goes, both deliver amazing performance from such tidy cases. The .300 WSM has the higher case capacity and is the faster of the pair, but it's important to understand that at some point

cartridge design cannot overcome case capacity. Both cartridges are close to .300 Win. Mag. performance, especially with 150-grain bullets, but there's a bit of a gap with 180-grain bullets, and if you wish to use even heavier bullets, the gap starts to widen.

I have both of these cartridges, and they're great. If you place a premium on performance in a shorter, lighter package, then they have much to offer. For me, however, if I go into fast .30 territory, I want a bit more velocity, and I want to wring

With newer propellants, .300 Win. Mag. velocity is creeping up. This Barnes Vortex load with 165-grain TTSX clocked 3,261 fps from a 24-inch barrel.

FAST .30 COMPARISON							
Cartridge	Manufacturer/ Bullet	Bullet Weight (gr.)	Muzzle Velocity (fps)	Muzzle Energy (ft.-lbs.)	Trajectory (in.)		
					100 yd.	300 yd.	400 yd.
.300 RCM	Hornady Superformance SST	150	3,310	3,648	1.1	-5.4	-16.0
.300 RCM	Hornady Superformance InterBond	180	3,040	3,693	1.4	-6.4	-18.5
.300 WSM	Winchester Ballistic Silvertip	150	3,300	3,628	1.1	-5.4	-15.9
.300 WSM	Federal Nosler AccuBond	180	2,980	3,500	1.5	-6.6	-19.0
.300 H&H	Hornady InterBond	180	2,900	3,361	1.6	-7.1	-20.7
.300 WIN. MAG.	Winchester Power-Point	150	3,290	3,605	1.3	-6.3	-19.0
.300 WIN. MAG.	Black Hills Nosler AccuBond	180	3,000	3,597	1.4	-6.5	-18.7
.300 WIN. MAG.	Hornady Superformance SST	180	3,130	3,917	1.3	-5.9	-17.3
.300 WBY. MAG.	Weatherby Nosler Partition	150	3,540	4,173	1.0	-4.9	-14.6
.300 WBY. MAG.	Weatherby Barnes TTSX	180	3,190	4,067	1.2	-5.6	-16.2
.300 WBY. MAG.	Federal Trophy Bonded Tip	180	3,100	3,840	1.4	-6.4	-18.7
.300 REM. ULTRA MAG	Remington Swift Scirocco	150	3,450	3,964	0.9	-4.9	-14.3
.300 REM. ULTRA MAG	Remington Swift Scirocco	180	3,250	4,221	1.1	-5.4	-15.6

NOTES: Velocity, energy and trajectory figures are factory-published. Trajectory figures based on 200-yard zero.

it out of heavier bullets. So let's keep looking.

LONG MAGNUMS

I love the old .300 H&H. Its archaic tapered case feeds like a dream, and it is steeped in class and nostalgia. If you're a handloader, you can wring surprising velocity out of that old-fashioned case, but today factory loads are few and all are anemic. Hell, there are .30-06 loads almost as fast as the current 180-grain .300 H&H load at 2,880 fps. We must pass.

Historically, my default has been the .300 Wby. Mag. It wasn't Roy Weatherby's personal favorite, but it has been and remains Weatherby's flagship cartridge. I got my first one, a Weatherby Mark V, back in about 1981. In the nineties, I started using a Rifles Inc. .300 Wby. on a Model 70 action—it's the rifle I used to take the Suleiman markhor shown in the lead photograph for this chapter—and lately I've been using a .300 Wby. barrel on a Blaser R8. Over the years these two rifles have accounted for the majority of my Asian mountain game, along with a lot of other stuff.

Norma has long loaded Weatherby's ammo, and it's fast—so fast it's pretty hard to get handloads up to that level. Most everybody loads .300 Wby. Mag. ammo today, and you can count on a 180-grain bullet cooking along at 3,150 fps or so.

The .300 Rem. Ultra Mag is almost certainly a better cartridge. Based on the .404 Jeffery case necked down, it's an unbelted case with a rebated rim, and it has more case capacity than the .300 Wby. With handloads or factory loads other than Weatherby, the Ultra Mag—the fully loaded version, as opposed to the lower power levels Remington offers for the cartridge—is probably 100 fps faster, and its cartridge design, at least in theory, is conducive to better accuracy. From what I see out there, it's starting to gain a bit in popularity, but it does bring us back to a single source for ammo, Remington, which is also the primary source for production rifles.

If you're going into fast .30 territory and you want fast .30 performance, both the .300 Wby. and the .300 Ultra Mag are exceedingly sound choices. I've used the Weatherby much more than the Ultra Mag, but I've gotten great accuracy out of

Critters such as the Punjab urial are tough and often engaged at longer ranges in rugged country. These are the conditions in which fast .30s such as the .300 Wby. Mag. excel.

both, and of course, the downrange performance is awesome.

Their drawbacks are shared. Both require a full-length (.375 H&H) action, and both need a 26-inch barrel to really strut their stuff. Together these mean a lightweight mountain rifle ain't gonna happen, but considering the recoil, I'm not sure you really want one.

So if the short magnums aren't quite enough and the super-fast long-actions are maybe a bit much, what is just right? In terms of cartridge design, the .300 Win. Mag. is all wrong. Its belted case, which was much in vogue when it was introduced in 1963, is now out of fashion.

Any rifle guy knows a proper rifle cartridge needs a full-caliber neck to properly grip the bullet. Apparently, the Winchester engineers didn't know this because when they necked down the .338 Win. Mag. case they lengthened the body and shortened the neck to .264 inch, maximizing case capacity. At first the howls about this horrible design deficiency were quite loud, but the .300 Win. Mag. seems to have survived. It isn't just the most popular .30 caliber magnum; it is the most popular cartridge to wear the "magnum" suffix.

Case design is a contributing factor to accuracy, but it is not anywhere near as important as a good barrel and good ammo. The .300 Win. Mag. has been popular with military snipers since the first Gulf War. They have no issues with its accuracy, nor does anyone else. Availability isn't everything, but in that aspect, the .300 Win. Mag. has no close second. Bob Forker's Ammo & Ballistics lists more than 70 factory loads, and it's offered by everyone.

The .300 Win. Mag. can be housed in a standard-length (.30-06) action, and it does just fine with a 24-inch barrel. It cannot be made as light or as short as a short .30 caliber magnum, but it offers a good compromise. And it performs.

For years the "standard" .300 Win. Mag. velocity has been 2,960 fps with a 180-grain bullet. That sounds kind of ho-hum compared to the Weatherby and Remington Ultra Mag, but with modern powders there are now a few factory loads and plenty of load recipes that exceed 3,000 fps. Hornady's Superformance 180-grain SST load is rated at 3,130 fps, which is similar to what both Hornady's and Federal's 180-grain .300 Wby. Mag. load will do. I checked the 180-grain Superformance load on my chronograph, and I was getting nearly 3,180 fps from a Legendary Arms Works .300 Win. Mag. That's deep into realistic .300 Wby. Mag. territory and clearly plenty of velocity.

I've had a couple of .300 Win. Mag. rifles, but generally it's a cartridge I've tried to avoid. Like I said, I've been a .300 Wby. guy. Because of its popularity, however, the .300 Win. Mag. is an unavoidable cartridge, so I've tested a lot of guns so chambered and, collectively, shot quite a bit of game with it. Over the years I have found it consistently accurate, but the past few months I've been using it more than ever because Legendary Arms Works is a sponsor of "The Boddington Experience" TV series, so I've dragged that .300 all over the place.

An equally good reason is that Kenny Jarrett sent me one of his Ridge Walkers in .300 Win. Mag. to play with. Initially, I thought they were pretty much equal in accuracy, but as the Jarrett barrel breaks in it's starting to pull ahead. I haven't been able to do any hunting with this rifle yet, but I look forward to it.

Honestly, for sheer versatility almost anywhere there isn't much you can't do with a fast .30 caliber and a 180-grain bullet. There aren't any bad choices to be made. If it's important to go light, the short magnums are the way to go. If absolute maximum performance is your deal, then it's the Weatherby or the Ultra Mag.

But what is the real bottom line? Remember, I'm a .300 Wby. guy, so I never thought I'd say this. But if you want fast .30 performance, you might as well just get a .300 Win. Mag. and be done with it. Sheer availability is one reason, but there's more. The .300 Win. Mag. is the compromise: a hair's breadth behind the long magnums in performance, able to be built into a lighter rifle, and no issues with accuracy. I probably should have figured that out years ago.

GOING BIG
IN NORTH AMERICA

IF YOU THOUGHT THE .375 WAS AN AFRICA-ONLY CALIBER, YOU'D BETTER THINK AGAIN.

by Craig Boddington

We were walking slowly down a trail, the wind in our faces, when a nilgai bull stepped out of an oak motte off to our left and advanced into the clearing. At that moment we were behind a mesquite, and he didn't see us. This is rare. Introduced into the Gulf Coast of South Texas more than 80 years ago, these big, short-horned antelope have keen senses and are extremely wary. In this area, where whitetails are carefully managed, the nilgai are actually spookier than the deer. So this bull was a gift. He was a good bull, big-bodied, dark in color, with thick horns starting to wear at the tips. Ryan Foster slowly set up the sticks, and I took the shot when the bull stopped at about 60 yards, quartering slightly to me.

He dropped in his tracks and stayed down. This, too, is a bit unusual. Nilgai are at least as tough as they are wary. A nilgai bull weighs 600 pounds and more. He's hard to put down and even harder to track because the thick, elastic skin tends to slip over a bullet wound, allowing little blood to escape. That this one dropped so readily wasn't a huge surprise because I hit him well with a 300-grain bullet from a .375 H&H.

For many hunters, the .375 H&H is synonymous with African safaris, but it's suitable for a lot more than that. First, a little history. The .375 H&H was not the original cartridge in that bullet diameter. It was preceded by the mild 9.5mm Mannlicher and the Holland & Holland .400/.375 Nitro Express, a long-forgotten cartridge that was the first belted cartridge, albeit a weak and unpopular one. Holland & Holland tried again in 1912 with the larger-cased and much faster .375 H&H Magnum.

I'm not sure what Holland & Holland expected the cartridge to be used for. It was obviously too big for game in England. But in 1912 the British Empire was at its height, and in those days India was the largest market for the British gun trade. Was it designed for very large game, or was it intended to become the champion of versatility it achieved? Evidence suggests the latter, since it was introduced with three bullet weights: a light, fast 235-grain bullet; and the two weights that remain most common today, 270 and 300 grains.

I would never suggest the .375 serves as an all-around North American cartridge, but it's obviously powerful enough for anything we have and yet actually shoots flat enough to be used effectively in most situations. I was in my late teens when I got my first .375, and I used it quite a bit, including game it wasn't ideally suited for: caribou, mule deer, pronghorn and sheep. Based on this, I can tell you it not only hits with authority, but on smaller animals produces relatively little bullet damage.

The .375 H&H is not only the granddaddy of the clan, but also by far the most popular of all .375 caliber cartridges. One could argue its tapered case and gentle shoulder are anachronisms, and its 2.8-inch case requires a full-length action. On the other hand, it's an accurate cartridge and extremely available. Everybody loads for the .375 H&H, so there are lots of choices in factory loads and also a century's worth of handload recipes.

Obviously there are .375s other than the H&H. Starting at the bottom, back in 1978 Winchester introduced the .375 Win. in a version of the Model 94 called the 94 Big Bore. The .375 Win. is reminiscent of the old .38-55 but quite a bit more powerful—propelling a 250-grain bullet at 1,900 fps and a light-for-caliber 200-grain bullet at 2,200 fps. Never popular and barely hanging on, it's a good cartridge for wild boar and black bear at close range. Just remember that bullets designed for the .375 Win. are not intended for use at .375 H&H velocities.

Hornady has developed two .375 caliber cartridges. First was the .376 Steyr, introduced in 2000. The .376 is a slightly rebated-rim cartridge with a 2.35-inch case loosely developed from the European 9.3x64mm case. Developed for the Steyr Scout Rifle, the .376 has not been popular, but it's a good cartridge—especially for North America.

Hornady offers both 225- and 270-grain loads at 2,600 fps. Obviously, the lighter bullets could be pushed faster, but bullet weight for bullet weight, the .376 Steyr lags about 100 fps behind the .375 H&H and thus kicks noticeably less. You give up a bit of power or a bit of range, but it's plenty of gun for anything in North America, and it fits into a .30-06-length action.

Introduced in 2006, the .375 Ruger is quite a different deal. It's an unbelted cartridge with a rim and base diameter of .532 inch, the same as a standard belted magnum, with a case length of 2.58 inches. Although

it fits into standard actions, the case has little taper and holds a lot of powder. Also, it gets a little extra bit of efficiency as a short, fat case.

The design criterion for Hornady's engineers was to equal the .375 H&H in the shorter case and achieve full velocity from a 22-inch barrel. They actually exceeded this goal. The .375 Ruger runs about 100 fps faster than the H&H, even if comparing a 24-inch barrel for the H&H against a 22-inch barrel for the Ruger.

The .375 Ruger can be housed in a more compact package than the H&H, and since it fits into standard actions, it can also be made more inexpensively—good examples being Ruger's Hawkeye and Mossberg's Patriot. I like the .375 Ruger a lot but since it's a bit faster than the H&H, it is also going to produce more recoil. This is not too obvious in rifles of equal weight, but a .375 Ruger rifle is often made lighter than the average H&H. You're gonna feel it.

Then there are the fast .375s: .375 Wby. Mag., .375 Rem. Ultra Mag and .378 Wby. Mag. Also, there are a slew of fast .375 wildcats like the .375 Ackley Improved, which is similar to the .375 Wby. Mag. in that both are based on the .375 H&H case, blown out to remove body taper and with sharper shoulders. Velocity gains over the H&H range from 100 to 200 fps.

For North American hunting, these faster .375s have the advantage of flatter trajectories and thus simplified shooting at longer ranges. Their primary issue is that recoil goes up exponentially as velocity increases. These cartridges really need to be

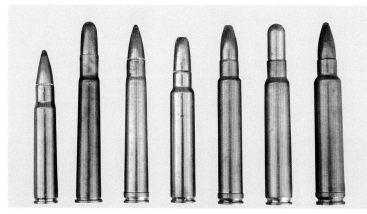

From l.: .376 Steyr, .375 H&H Flanged, .375 H&H, .375 Ruger, .375 Wby. Mag., .375 Rem. Ultra Mag, .378 Wby. Mag. As you move to the right, trajectories get considerably flatter, but recoil goes up dramatically.

.375 BALLISTICS COMPARISON

Cartridge	Bullet	BULLET WEIGHT (gr.)	MUZZLE VELOCITY (fps)	MUZZLE ENERGY (ft.-lbs.)	TRAJECTORY 300 YD. (in.)	400 YD. (in.)
.30-06	Black Hills Nosler AB	180	2,700	2,915	-8.6	-24.6
.270 WIN.	Hornady SST	130	3,060	2,702	-6.3	-18.5
.376 STEYR	Hornady SP	225	2,600	3,377	-10.6	-31.5
.376 STEYR	Hornady InterLock	270	2,600	4,052	-9.9	-28.9
.375 H&H	Hornady InterLock	270	2,700	4,370	-9.2	-26.0
.375 H&H	Hornady InterLock SF	270	2,800	4,699	-8.3	-24.3
.375 RUGER	Hornady GMX	250	2,900	4,668	-7.3	-21.7
.375 RUM	Remington Swift A-Frame	300	2,760	5,073	-8.8	-26.1
.375 RUM	Nosler AccuBond	260	2,950	5,023	-6.9	-19.9
.375 WBY. MAG.	Weatherby Nosler Part.	300	2,800	5,224	-8.2	-24.0
.378 WBY. MAG.	Weatherby Barnes X	270	3,150	6,030	-5.8	-16.7
.378 WBY. MAG.	Nosler AccuBond	260	3,000	5,195	-6.6	-19.1

NOTES: Factory ballistics. Trajectories based on 200-yard zero. Abbreviations: AB, AccuBond; Part., Partition; SF, Superformance; SP, spire point

The .376 Steyr is not a cartridge you hear a lot about, but it's a versatile round suitable for big game like muskox.

tamed with muzzle brakes, with the attendant cost in muzzle blast. Realistically, we don't have anything in North America that really needs to be hit that hard, and the game we have that is most appropriate to a .375 is not normally taken at longer ranges.

The most obvious application for the .375 is our biggest bears. Alaskan brown and polar bears are both as big as Cape buffalo and just as tough, but there is potential for 200-yard shooting. A fast .33 or .35 will do the job and the case can be argued for a .416, but the .375 is just about right. I used a .375 H&H on my first brown bear in 1981, and in 2015 I shot a big polar bear with a Mossberg Patriot in .375 Ruger.

The argument isn't as strong with grizzly bears and even less with black bears. They are not as big, and depending on area and hunting technique, shooting distances can be a bit farther. A fast .33 with a 250-grain bullet might be a slightly better choice for grizzly. On the other hand, a really big grizzly can weigh a half-ton, and while the average black bear may weigh 200 pounds, we all hope for an outsized quarter-ton bear, and

When the biggest bears are on the menu, the .375s make a lot of sense. Boddington killed this polar bear with a Mossberg Patriot chambered to .375 Ruger.

black bears over 800 pounds have been recorded. I've used .375s on grizzly, and I've taken a number of black bears with .375s. No apologies: The .375 really thumps a bear, any bear.

Beyond bears, the genuine suitability of a .375 in North America is sketchy. The .375 is marvelously effective on moose but really isn't needed. With lighter bullets pushed fast, a .375 is awesome on elk, but it also isn't needed. Then there are less commonly hunted species, such as bison, muskox and walrus, along with the aforementioned nilgai and a few other introduced species like sambar and water buffalo also found on our continent.

On the bovines and biggest bears, traditional 300-grain .375 bullets intended for very large game are just fine. It doesn't matter whether they're roundnose or spitzer because shots are generally close and all of these were designed with large game in mind.

For general North American use—and for use on lighter game—there are other options. First, you need to get past the roundnose design in order to make the best use of whatever velocity your .375 achieves. Two of my favorites have been Hornady's 270-grain InterLock spire point and Sierra's 300-grain GameKing, a boattail spitzer.

You can go even lighter. Over the years I've used Speer's 235-grain Hot-Cor quite a bit. With modern powders you can get it up to nearly 3,100 fps in the H&H. However, this bullet weight is so much lighter than standard that accuracy suffers in some rifles. The Barnes 235-grain Triple Shock bullet may provide better accuracy than a lead-core bullet because it's longer.

Lighter bullets do produce a lot less recoil for practice as well. Hornady's 225-grain semi-spitzer designed for the .376 Steyr is great for low-recoil practice in the faster .375s, and on

ACCURACY AND CONSISTENCY

Large calibers are often very accurate. There is a reason. A few ten-thousandths of fouling or slight imperfections in the bore or on the bullet are proportionately less significant in, say, a .375 than in cartridges of lesser caliber. I have found all the .375s to be very accurate. However, this is mitigated by recoil—which makes shooting tight groups more difficult—and also by the low-powered scopes we often use on larger calibers. Recoil is what it is, but on .375s for general use, these days I usually mount a larger, more versatile scope such as a 2-7X or 3-9X.

The legend of the .375, especially the H&H, is it tends to shoot multiple bullet weights into the same group. Yes, it is a forgiving caliber, but it's not magical. Some .375s shoot a variety of loads into the same 100-yard group, but others do not, so don't count on it.

To prove the point, I fired two groups consisting of a random selection of six .375 H&H loads with bullet weights varying from 260 to 300 grains from two rifles of similar accuracy. One group measured just over two inches—very consistent—but the other group, using the exact same six loads, measured over seven inches.—*CB*

deer-size game the light bullets hit like lightning striking.

For more general use, Nosler makes a 260-grain .375 in both AccuBond and Partition. Both kick less than standard .375 bullet weights, can be pushed faster and should be considered at least "bear capable." I've used the 260-grain AccuBond quite a bit, and it's effective.

In addition to its old 235-grain Hot-Cor, Speer also has a 270-grain boattail spitzer, so you get the velocity with a bit better velocity retention. The company also has a 285-grain Grand Slam bullet, easily suitable for the biggest bears and anything else. The Barnes Triple Shocks in both 270 and 300 grains are spitzer designs, so both hold their velocity well.

Across the caliber spectrum the toughness of homogeneous-alloy bullets allows one to reduce weight (and recoil) and increase velocity without sacrificing penetration. This makes the Barnes 235-grain bullet interesting. It also offers a 250-grain bullet, and Hornady has a new 250-grain GMX.

When I chose the .375 Ruger for polar bear, obviously an important hunt, I had a dilemma. Some shots are close when bears come into camp to eat the occupants, but other shots must be taken at some distance to prevent a bear from getting into open leads or pressure ridges. With this in mind, I chose the Hornady 250-grain GMX. At 2,900 fps in the .375 Ruger, it's fast, flat-shooting and certain to penetrate. My shot was at about 45 yards. I shot three times to ensure the bear was anchored and stayed anchored, and all three bullets exited. You can't ask for more.

THE WONDERFUL
WHELEN

THE SURPRISINGLY VERSATILE .35 WHELEN CARTRIDGE SOLDIERS ON.

by Layne Simpson

Before taking a close look at the .35 Whelen, it might be appropriate to first settle a seemingly ongoing argument about who originated it. Some believe it was James V. Howe; the opposing team favors his boss, Townsend Whelen. Ignored is the fact that Whelen himself settled the debate in a couple of his books long before it started.

Whelen's *The Hunting Rifle* was published during the early 1940s, and page 271 reads as follows: "In 1922 Mr. James V. Howe and the writer developed the .400 Whelen cartridge. This cartridge was constructed by taking the .30-06 case before it had been necked at all and necking it down to .40 caliber. About the time we completed development of this cartridge I went on a long hunting trip in the Northwest, and when I returned Mr. Howe showed me another cartridge which he had developed. The .30-06 case was necked to .35 caliber to use existing .35 caliber bullets. Mr. Howe asked my permission to call this cartridge the .35 Whelen, but he alone deserves credit for its development."

Whelen's book on reloading, *Why Not Load Your Own!*, was published

in 1957. In the section on the .35 Whelen he writes, "This cartridge was developed by James V. Howe in 1922, and named for the writer."

I have read a lot of Whelen's work, and he always struck me as an extremely modest man. But he was also known for his painstakingly accurate reporting, and had he been involved in the creation of the cartridge bearing his name, he surely would have written so.

Col. Whelen was the commanding officer at Frankford Arsenal in Philadelphia during the 1920s. Howe, a talented gunsmith, was in charge of the machine shop tool room. Upon leaving Frankford in 1923, Howe got together with cabinetmaker Seymour Griffin and formed a custom rifle shop called Griffin & Howe. But the partnership was short-lived, and Howe ended up at Hoffman Arms Company in Cleveland, Ohio, where he stayed for many years.

Leslie Simpson, who was considered to be an American authority on hunting the African continent, also played a role in the creation of the .35 Whelen. Among many other adventures, he along with novelist Stewart Edward White bagged more

than 50 lions on a control shoot. During a conversation with Whelen in 1921, Simpson mentioned using the .35 Win. with less than satisfactory results.

He went on to say the ideal cartridge for use on thin-skinned game, including lion, was a .35 caliber cartridge pushing a 250-grain bullet at 2,500 to 2,600 fps. Shortly thereafter, Whelen mentioned the conversation to Howe. Sometime after developing the .35 Whelen, Howe followed up with the .350 Griffin & Howe Mag.

During the 1920s and into the 1930s, the .35 Whelen enjoyed considerable popularity among American hunters. This is mainly because until the Winchester Model 70 in .375 H&H Mag. was introduced in 1937, rifles chambered for a medium-bore cartridge suitable for use on large and potentially dangerous game were scarce.

At the time, Mauser sporting rifles and rifles built by several British firms were being imported, but all were quite expensive when compared to those made in the United States. Griffin & Howe began offering custom rifles in .375 H&H during the 1920s, but they also were a bit rich for the working-man. Coming up with a rifle in .35 Whelen was as simple and inexpen-

With the right twist rate, the Whelen can handle the full range of .35 bullets. From l.: Barnes TTSX 180 grains, Barnes TSX 200, Barnes TSX 225, Sierra boattail 225, Speer Grand Slam 250, Swift A-Frame 250, Woodleigh Weldcore 275, Swift A-Frame 285, Barnes 300 (discontinued) and Woodleigh Weldcore 310.

SIMPSON'S FAVORITE .35 WHELEN LOADS

Bullet	Bullet Weight (gr.)	Powder Type	Powder Charge (gr.)	Muzzle Velocity (fps)	Standard Deviation (fps)	Avg. Group (in.)
WOODLEIGH WELDCORE	310	RL 15	52.0	2,236	23	0.95
BARNES TSX FB	180	RL 15	60.0	2.832	16	1.12
SIERRA GAMEKING	225	VV N140	57.0	2,675	22	1.15
WOODLEIGH WELDCORE	310	W 748	53.0	2,271	15	1.18
REMINGTON CORE-LOKT	200	n/a	n/a	2,639	33	1.23
SPEER GRAND SLAM	250	VV N140	55.0	2,438	12	1.35
BARNES TSX FB	225	RL 15	57.0	2,761	18	1.38
SWIFT A-FRAME	250	RL 15	55.0	2,514	19	1.42
WOODLEIGH WELDCORE	275	RL 15	54.0	2,352	26	1.44
HORNADY INTERLOCK	200	n/a	n/a	2,962	29	1.55
FEDERAL TB BEAR CLAW	225	n/a	n/a	2,760	48	1.65
SWIFT A-FRAME	280	RL 15	54.0	2,383	17	1.61
BARNES ORIGINAL	300	RL 15	53.0	2,255	11	1.74
REMINGTON PSP	250	n/a	n/a	2,386	19	1.74

NOTES: Test rifle is a custom '98 Mauser with 22-inch Apex barrel, Redfield 1-4X scope. N/A indicates factory load. Powder charges are maximum and should be reduced by 10 percent for starting loads. Hornady cases and Federal GM205M primers were used. Accuracy results are averages of three three-shot groups at 100 yards. Velocities are averages of nine rounds clocked 12 feet from the muzzle by an Oehler Model 33 chronograph. Abbreviations: FB, flat base; RL, Reloder; TB, Trophy Bonded; VV, Vihtavouri; W, Winchester

sive as switching barrels on a rifle in .30-06.

Big-bore guy Elmer Keith was a promoter of the .400 Whelen cartridge and used it in a custom rifle given to him by Howe in 1925. The case had very little shoulder area, which made the cartridge troublesome to reload and shoot, so Keith eventually had his rifle rebarreled to .35 Whelen.

He used it to take what was described as a record-book brown bear on his first hunt in Alaska in 1937. His handload consisted of a 275-grain bullet made by Western Tool & Copper Company seated atop a maximum charge of IMR 4064 powder.

When writing about the cartridge, Keith opined that a 300-grain bullet made by Fred Barnes, who founded Barnes Bullets, might be a better choice for "raking shots" on elk in dark timber, but whether or not he actually got around to using it is not known.

Through the years Remington has been a leader in the domestication of wildcat cartridges, so the 1988 introduction of .35 Whelen ammunition in green boxes and the designation stamped on the barrels of Model 700 and Model 7600 rifles came as no surprise.

The 200-grain deer bullet at 2,675 fps shot about as flat as the .30-06 loaded with a 180-grain bullet. The 250-grain moose bullet was rated at 2,400 fps, and due to its round nose, its trajectory was only slightly better than that of a bowling ball. The fact that it was chosen over the 250-grain Pointed Core-Lokt previously loaded by Remington in the .350 Rem. Mag. was a big disappointment among fans of the .35 Whelen.

In those days people wrote letters, and the company obviously received a few because the blunt-nosed bullet was eventually replaced by one with a pointed nose for a big improvement in both trajectory and downrange energy delivery.

Remington continues to offer those same two loads, and there are a number of others. (See the accompanying chart for details.) Hornady Superformance with a 200-grain softpoint rated at 2,920 fps is the speed demon of the bunch. When

my Oehler Model 33 indicated 2,962 fps from a 22-inch barrel, I figured old faithful needed new batteries or was on the blink. So I retrieved a backup Model 33 from the truck and five bullets screamed across its screens at a 2,974 fps average. That's an honest 200 fps faster than the Remington 200-grain load and more than 100 fps faster than 180-grain handloads in my rifle.

I have not hunted with the Hornady ammo, but it should be quite deadly on deer. A moose, elk and bear load with a 225-grain GMX at 2,800 fps would be a nice addition to the Superformance family.

Handloading the .35 Whelen is a snap. Hornady and Remington offer unprimed cases, or they can be made by necking up .30-06 cases. A tapered expander button in full-length resizing dies made by Redding, RCBS, Hornady and others makes the job easy with no case loss during the process. It goes even more smoothly when a light coat of wax-type resizing lube available from Hornady and Redding is applied to the mouth of each case prior to the neck-up operation.

CURRENT .35 WHELEN FACTORY LOADS

Maker/Bullet	Bullet Weight (gr.)	Muzzle Velocity (fps)	Muzzle Energy (ft.-lbs.)	200 Yd. Energy (ft.-lbs.)	200 Yd. Drop* (in.)
BARNES VOR-TX TTSX FB	180	2,900	3,362	2,112	-3.7
BARNES VOR-TX TTSX BT	200	2,700	3,238	2,216	-4.3
FEDERAL FUSION	200	2,800	3,481	2,327	-3.9
HORNADY SUPERFORMANCE	200	2,910	3,760	2,303	-3.7
NOSLER CUSTOM ACCUBOND	200	2,700	3,237	2,204	-4.3
REMINGTON CORE-LOKT	200	2,675	3,177	1,958	-4.7
FEDERAL TB BEAR CLAW	225	2,600	3,377	2,238	-4.9
NOSLER ACCUBOND**	225	2,750	3,777	2,821	-3.8
NOSLER CUSTOM PARTITION	225	2,750	3,777	2,737	-3.9
REM. HIGH PERFORMANCE PSP	250	2,400	3,197	2,230	-5.7
NORMA ORYX	250	2,428	3,273	2,121	-5.7
NOSLER CUSTOM PARTITION	250	2,550	3,609	2,618	-4.8

NOTES: *Factory figures using 100-yard zero; Barnes 180-grain and Hornady factory figures use 200-yard zeroes, so these trajectories were recalculated based on 100-yard zero. **Available in Custom, Trophy Grade and Safari lines. Abbreviations: BT, boattail; FB, flat base; PSP, pointed softpoint; TB, Trophy Bonded

There are many great .35 Whelen powders and an abundance of good reloading manuals tells us how much of each to use. Among those I have tried, Vihtavuori N140, Hodgdon Varget, Accurate 2520, Winchester 748 and IMR 4064 have performed nicely. But if I could have only one sitting on the shelf in my reloading room, it would be Alliant Reloder 15. It burns cleanly, delivers top velocities with all bullets ranging from 180 to 310 grains in weight, flows through a good powder measure with minimum charge-to-charge variation, and maximum charges are either 100 percent density or close to it.

Neither is there a scarcity of great bullets. Those in the 225- to 250-grain range will handle everything from whitetails to Alaska-Yukon moose, but for those who wish to go the heavy-bullet route as preferred by Elmer Keith, there are excellent options weighing from 275 to 310 grains from Swift and Woodleigh.

Rifle availability is another story. Remington, the company that brought major manufacturer legitimacy to the Whelen, currently doesn't catalog a .35 Whelen. Nosler does in both the M48 Outfitter and M48 Heritage, but that's about it— which puts the cartridge in the custom or rebarrel/rechamber camp.

In the old days, the barrels of rifles in .35 Whelen usually had a 1:12 or 1:14 rifling twist rate, but when taking the .35 Whelen under wing, Remington chose to use 1:16 as previously used in rifles in .350 Rem. Mag. That's fine for some bullets, but the heavyweights need a quicker twist for stability in flight. A 1:14 twist is usually needed for the 275-grain Woodleigh and 280-grain Swift A-Frame while 1:12 is required for Woodleigh's 310-grain Weldcore.

I began hunting with the .35 Whelen back when it was still a wildcat and the barreled action of my favorite rifle was put together by Butch Searcy. On a square-bridge

'98 Mauser action, it wears one of Sam May's Apex barrels measuring 22 inches in length. Barnes 275- and 300-grain bullets were available, so I went with a 1:12 twist. Searcy machined a quarter rib to hold a folding rear sight and installed a banded ramp sight up front. The bolt shroud was modified for a Model 70-style safety.

The custom shop at E. C. Bishop & Son in Warsaw, Missouri, stocked the barreled action, and the only scope is has ever worn is a 1960s-vintage Redfield 1-4X variable. The scope is held in place by quick-detach rings made by the original Kimber of Oregon. The outfit weighs 8.5 pounds, and in addition to being quite comfortable to shoot, it is the most accurate rifle in .35 Whelen I have ever shot.

Since the beginning of the early 1900s, American hunters have had a dozen or so different .35 caliber rifle cartridges from which to choose, and with the exception of the .35 Rem. (which is none too healthy these days), most have been ignored to death.

The .35 Whelen has yet to win a popularity contest, but it is proving to be a survivor. During a hopefully short era when shooting game at shameful distances is all the rage among a small segment of the population, the .35 Whelen is kept alive by real hunters who have the ability to get closer before pulling the trigger.

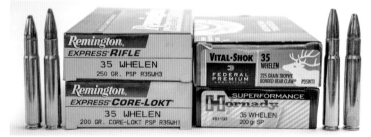

As the chart on the previous page shows, there's a surprising number of Whelen factory loads available, a testament to the cartridge's capabilities. It's a great North American big game round for those who prefer to get in relatively close.

PART II
CARTRIDGE DEEP-DIVE

M an, I almost forgot again. My old friend Tom Willoughby called and said he'd been seeing a good boar. If I was free that afternoon we could go look for him. Tom is one the most successful wild hog outfitters here on the Central Coast, so I scrambled. Hunting license, yes. Hog tag, yes. I opened the safe and reached for my .35 Whelen—and then stopped dead in my tracks. I didn't have any unleaded ammo for that rifle.

I live in what we call the "condor zone," a large chunk of California that has been declared "lead free" because of possible lead poisoning of endangered condors. All hunting must be done with lead-free projectiles. So I kept digging. Good grief, did I have anything sighted in for a legal load? Fortunately I did: a Blaser R8 in .300 Blaser Magnum that shoots 180-grain Barnes TTSX really well.

That afternoon we glassed a black pig bedded in a little depression on the shady side of a big, open ridge. He was about 225 yards away, with the slope such that we wouldn't be able to see him if we tried to get closer. Problem was, we couldn't tell what kind of pig it was, even with a spotting scope. The animal would have to stand up. So we waited, and with the light fading fast the hog finally stood, and Tom saw through the spotting scope that it was a good boar. I centered the shoulder and fired. The boar took off as if nothing had happened, but he faltered in a dozen yards and went down.

It must have been 25 years ago when Barnes Bullets' Randy Brooks chanced to be in the old Petersen Publishing offices in Los Angeles, where I was working at the time. He was already making the homogenous-alloy non-expanding bullet called the Super Solid, and he had prototypes, fired and unfired, for an expanding copper-alloy bullet with a nose cavity skived so that the expanded bullets showed consistent expansion in four opposing petals. Interesting. He intended to call it the Super Softpoint.

By Craig Boddington

GOING LEAD-FREE

What today's homogenous-alloy bullets offer the hunter, and tips on using them.

The expansion, though consistent, wasn't dramatic. It looked like a bullet that would be more of a penetrator than an expander, so I suggested that wasn't a very good name, as it seemed to imply massive and rapid expansion. We kicked it around a bit. With those characteristic four petals deployed, the bullet had a cross shape to the front. Or, if you turned it a bit, it made an "X." It was right there in my old office that the X Bullet received its name.

It was, in fact, a bullet that excelled in deep penetration. Since copper is less dense than lead, the bullet has to be a bit longer to reach the same weight. Over time we learned that we had to play with the loads a bit and seat the bullet deeper, but the X Bullet worked very well. It was also somewhat finicky: Some rifles liked it and others just hated it. It was also pure hell for copper fouling.

The next generation, the much more recent TSX or Triple Shock, made the bullet much less finicky and greatly reduced the fouling.

This was done through the simple expedient of grooves (the number depends on the caliber and bullet weight) turned into the shank of the bullet, creating driving bands.

The finicky nature of the X, at least in some measure, comes from the fact that a copper or copper alloy bullet isn't "compressible" like a lead-core bullet. There is a pressure spike as

The Barnes TTSX is the latest evolution of the X bullet. The tip helps initiate expansion while the grooves help with accuracy (and cleanliness).

These recovered .30 caliber Hornady GMX bullets were fired at descending velocities (left to right). There is more expansion at higher velocity, but the bullets function well across a broad velocity spectrum.

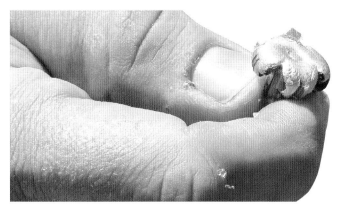

The new Power Core from Winchester, this one recovered from ballistic gelatin, shows the most expansion the author's ever seen from a homogenous-alloy bullet.

it takes the rifling, and some rifles didn't like it. The driving bands reduce friction, thus reducing the pressure spike, and it also reduces copper fouling. No bullet groups equally well in all rifles, but in my experience the TSX shoots at least reasonably well in most rifles, and exceptionally well in quite a few.

The TSX is still with us, but it's joined by a version with a polymer tip—actually a plug—inserted into the nose cavity. This is the TTSX, or Tipped Triple Shock. As is the case with a traditional lead core bullet, upon impact the polymer tip is driven into the nose of the bullet, promoting initial expansion. In my experience the TTSX thus seems to expand a bit faster than the Triple Shock.

The principles of the homogenous-alloy bullet—the Barnes and those that have followed— remain much the same: Upon impact, the nose opens and peels back, forming the classic petals. Although petals will occasionally flake or break off, because of the elasticity of the copper and the homogenous nature of the bullet they generally remain

intact—producing weight retention in the high 90 percent range.

The capability to expand is limited by the depth of the cavity. Essentially, the petals open to the depth of the cavity, and then they hit a wall. This is similar to the expansion of the Nosler Partition, which stops at the divider. However, because the petals only rarely break off and there is no lead to wipe off, weight retention is very high.

Over the years I have used the X, the TSX and the TTSX quite a bit. Especially with the latter two, the accuracy is usually pretty good and sometimes fantastic. Aside from component bullets from Barnes, Federal is the primary U.S. source for factory ammo with Barnes TSX and TTSX bullets, although Black Hills also loads Barnes bullets in its Gold line—along with several varmint offerings in its standard red box line.

Obviously the industry had a long opportunity to look at the X bullet and its successors. Remembering my early conversations with Randy Brooks, the X was designed to be a deep-penetrating hunting bullet that would

typically give nearly 100 percent weight retention. The fact that it happened to be lead-free was actually a byproduct, not a goal.

Politics can change things quickly. Restrictions such as my condor zone and other areas where lead cannot be used have led to the rapid introduction of other homogenous-alloy bullets. The concept already in place, developers of the new entries tweaked the alloy formulae and the placement of any grooves. The depth and diameter of the nose cavity, which I'm told is the most difficult manufacturing aspect of this type of bullet, can also be tweaked.

The point is, shooters who either must use lead-free bullets or who like their deep-penetrating characteristics now have choices. This is important because even within a fairly narrow type of bullet, no rifle shoots all bullets the same.

Since its introduction just two years ago I have used Hornady's GMX (Gilding Metal Expanding) quite a bit. This is a polymer-tipped bullet with two grooves. Accuracy has been consistently good. In my experience, which is pretty considerable now, expansion characteristics are very similar to the X-type bullet. Hornady is obviously the source for both loaded ammo and component bullets.

Much the same applies to Nosler's answer, the E-Tip ("E" for "eco-friendly"). The E-Tip is a cool-looking bullet with a green polymer tip, no grooves, and, as loaded by Winchester in its Supreme line, signature black coating. Component bullets from Nosler lack this coating.

I have only limited field experience with the Nosler E-Tip, one

Non-lead bullets are great for tough animals such as hogs where you need a lot of penetration but not always ideal for deer and other thin-skinned game.

elk and two sheep—all 150-grain 7mm bullets from a 7mm Remington Magnum. I had high hopes of recovering at least one bullet to admire and photograph, but all zipped right on through, showing only moderate expansion at the exit wounds—similar in performance to other homogenous-alloy bullets I've used. Accuracy has been very good.

For the guys who like exit wounds, through-and-through penetration, they are all very good choices. I think they come into their own on larger, tougher game where penetration becomes the most essential characteristic. For instance, last year in Greenland I wanted to use a CZ .270 on both reindeer and muskox. The .270 is perfect for reindeer but marginal for muskox. I hedged my bet with a Triple Shock bullet, and the muskox went nowhere.

In Turkey in the fall of '09, when the GMX was brand new, I had to borrow a rifle when my primary scope came apart. The rifle was my wife's .270, and the GMX grouped well in her gun. I shot a massive Anatolian stag at 400 yards. I shot him twice, the second unnecessary. He went nowhere, and the bullets exited.

Because of their toughness and the fact they lose almost no weight, homogenous-alloy bullets also break the rules about bullet weight. On both the muskox and the stag, I used 130-grain bullets with confidence; in a lead-core bullet I would have been much more comfortable with 150-grain slugs. This offers the ability to use a faster load with less recoil.

However, while they're ideal for large, tough game—and for pushing the caliber envelope as I did on the muskox—I don't think they offer quite enough expansion to be ideal for deer-sized game, which includes sheep, goats, pronghorn and so forth.

On game such as this, homogenous-alloy bullets will expand as much as they can, then they will penetrate and probably exit, expending a great deal of energy on the far side.

On thin-skinned big game with this type of bullet, perhaps the most important thing you can do is change your hold slightly. We Americans tend to prefer the lung shot. It offers the largest target, and our general rationale is that it destroys less meat than a shoulder shot. On deer-size game, an animal shot through the lungs with this type of bullet is probably going to cover a bit of ground. How far it goes will depend on where the hit was, the caliber and the character or mental state of that individual animal.

I have long had a theory that these homogenous-alloy bullets do most of their expansion very quickly. So especially on hits on bone and solid muscle, you often do see impressive initial impact—and then the bullet keeps going. On softer tissue, like behind the shoulder, this initial hard hit doesn't seem as pronounced.

So change your thinking and your hold. To get the very best performance from this type of bullet, instead of the behind-the-shoulder lung shot look for the center of the shoulder. The bullet will absolutely penetrate and probably still exit. The animal may or may not drop in its tracks, you never know, but when you hit heavy bone like that and then penetrate through to the vitals, an animal is unlikely to go very far.

As for meat loss, this type of bullet is actually much less destructive than most lead-core bullets. Because of limited expansion, the wound channel is narrower, and there is very little fragmentation. Bone fragments do become secondary projectiles, but a lot of the time you can "eat right up to the bullet hole."

As I said, I think the deep-penetrating type of homogenous-alloy bullet is pretty close to perfection, but there's room for improvement. For instance, Remington's Copper Solid is a tipped bullet with a larger cavity that promises 1.8-times-caliber expansion. I haven't used it yet.

And then there's Winchester's new Power Core unleaded bullet, just now being released. It's part of the Super-X standard line of ammo, so it won't come at a big price premium. The other thing that's exciting about it is the Power Core was designed as a deer bullet, with expansion characteristics similar to the good old Power Point.

Also called the "95/5"—a copper alloy of 95 percent copper—it has a larger, deeper, contoured nose cavity. Demonstrations I've seen in ballistic gelatin show that it actually does produce dramatic expansion, more than I've seen in any homogenous alloy bullet.

Note, please, that you can't have everything in one bullet: The greater expansion limits penetration, so it cannot and will not penetrate as well as the Barnes, Nosler and Hornady non-lead offerings. Which goes right back to basic questions we must all answer when choosing bullets: What game are you hunting? What kind of performance are you looking for? Where do you like to place your shots? As time goes on, I predict our choices in lead-free bullets will increase, as will their performance parameters.

GUIDE TO BIG GAME BULLETS

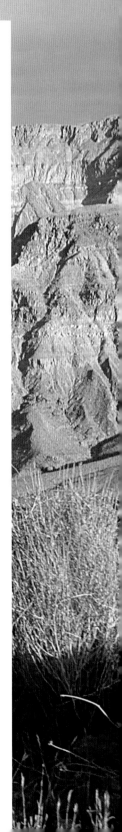

Our man gives you the ultimate bullet selection plan.

By Craig Boddington

Campfire cartridge controversy is lots of fun, and we all have our favorites, but there are lots of popular calibers that are actually pretty darned close in diameter. It's a very subtle progression as you go from, say, .257 to .264 or from .277 to .284. How many of us can tell at a glance a bullet that is just .007 inch fatter than another? (Wait, let me get my glasses on!)

With diameters so similar, there are a lot of calibers—and cartridges within the calibers—that are virtually identical in effect on game. Most of our campfire arguments are based largely on personal preference (based on limited personal experience) and, from a purely objective viewpoint, are pretty thin. But there is one irrefutable concept: Regardless of the caliber or the cartridge, it's always the bullet that does the work.

I've hunted with virtually all of the popular bullet diameters, generally multiple cartridges in each. My word isn't law on the subject, but my purpose here is to offer my preferred big game bullet weights in the popular hunting calibers.

.244

In my view there's good reason why .22 centerfires are illegal for big game in many states. They are, however, legal in some. I've seen deer taken very cleanly with the little .22 Hornet, and I've taken quite a few with the .223 and .22-250. It really is a matter of shot placement, and if you stick to head and neck shots, any 50- to 55-grain bullet will drop deer as if struck by lightning. However, not all of us have the discipline to limit ourselves to such shots, and we have to keep in mind that most .224-inch bullets weren't designed to provide adequate penetration on deer-size game. So if you insist on using such a light cartridge, stick with bullets of 60 grains and higher that were designed as deer bullets. Even with such bullets, game should be limited to javelina, pronghorns and small to mid-size deer.

6mm/.243

Most bullets of 95 grains and higher were intended as big game bullets; most lighter ones are fast-opening varmint bullets. The most popular and most common is by far the 100-grain bullet, and it's a great choice for pronghorn and deer. There are slightly heavier 6mm bullets and also very tough bullets, and some folks use them for game up to elk. I prefer not to. At medium range the 6mms are adequate for any deer that walks, but they are extremely marginal for elk.

.257

My friend and editor Scott Rupp, a fan of the .25s, likes to remind me that this caliber isn't my cup of tea. I've used the .250 Savage a bit, and the .25-06 and .257 Weatherby a bit more, and I even used the almost late, lamented .25 WSSM. The .25s are awesome for deer and, while I don't think of any .25 as an elk rifle, they are used often enough that it's silly to question such application.

I tend to think of the .25 as the lightest caliber that should be used for general North America big game—excluding moose and big bears. There are some 100-grain slugs that make very good deer bullets, but I much prefer (and have generally used) heavier bullets in the 115- to 120-grain range.

6.5mm/.264

I'm not crazy about the .25s because their ballistic coefficients don't hold up as well in wind as calibers from 6.5mm on up do. For instance, while Speer's 120-grain .25 boattail spitzer has a BC of .480, most .25 caliber spitzers are down in the high .300 range. By contrast, most 6.5 spitzers of similar weight range from the high .400s to the low .500s. This is a considerable difference, and it shows up quickly when the wind blows.

Bullets in 6.5mm are also available with considerably heavier (and heavier-for-caliber) bullets, which translates to higher sectional density and thus greater penetration. So for me, the 6.5mm is the lightest caliber that makes sense for the general run of big game hunting.

I've hunted quite a bit with the .260 Remington and .264 Winchester Magnum. I've done 1,000-yard shooting with the 6.5mm Creedmoor, and I just did some African hunting with an old 6.5x53R. I've also used wildcats and proprietaries, including the 6.5-.284, 6.5-06 and Lazzeroni's sizzling 6.71 (.264) Blackbird.

With modern bullets, the 140-grain 6.5mm is a great choice for larger game and general use.

For the big bears, you obviously want a heavy-for-caliber, tough bullet. This Kamchatka bear fell to a 250-grain Nosler Partition from a .340 Weatherby Magnum.

The .243 and .257 are great for small big game, but their relatively low ballistic coefficients mean they drift more in the wind, which hurts them at long range.

I have used the traditional, old 160-grain bullet, but except for very specialized purposes there isn't a need: The 140-grain bullet will do it all.

That said, in more open country I have traditionally used somewhat lighter bullets. When I was a kid I had a .264 that I thought was the cat's pajamas. I always shot the old 129-grain Hornady Spire Point, and it was (and is) fast and flat. Today Hornady offers the same bullet weight in both SST and Inter-Bond (BC .485) and Nosler has a 130-grain AccuBond (BC .488).

For game smaller than elk, these are great choices in the fast 6.5s.

In smaller cases such as the .260 and Creedmoor, well, you can't get fancy velocity anyway, so the tried-and-true 140s are probably better choices. However, bullet construction does matter. I live in a lead-free zone in California, and I've been astonished by the performance of 120-grain Barnes TSX in the little .260 Remington.

.277

I first used a .270 back in the 1970s. Jack O'Connor was a 130-grain guy in his beloved .270s. Being more of a heavy-bullet fan, and also a bit contrary, I used 150-grain bullets. That rifle was stolen in the early 1980s, and it was some years before I returned to the .270. By then the compromise 140-grain bullet was available, and it has been and remains my favorite bullet weight—whether in .270 Winchester, .270 WSM or .270 Weath-

erby Magnum, all of which I've used quite a bit.

Having stated my preference, I should say further it is really simple with this caliber: It doesn't much matter. The three common bullet weights of 130, 140 and 150 grains are all just fine for everything from deer and sheep up to elk and black bear. I've used all three of these weights to kill elk and elk-size game—both close and far—with no problems whatsoever. The 130s are faster. Given similar shape and construction, the 150s penetrate better. The 140s are a great compromise. Take your pick.

7mm/.284

While I much prefer either the .270 or the .30 caliber, I have hunted with almost all of the factory 7mm cartridges. My favorite is the good old 7x57, but I've used the 7mm Remington Magnum more than all the rest put together.

7mm bullets designed for big game probably start at 120 grains and go up to 175 grains. For my tastes, the 120s are too light for the caliber. The 175s offer wonderful penetration, but even in the large-cased 7mms they're slow—and with the great bullets we have today I don't think they are necessary.

So depending on the cartridge, the 7mm bullets I prefer run from 140 to 165 grains. In slower cartridges such as the 7x57 and 7mm-08 I generally use 140-grain bullets, and they work wonderfully.

I have used this bullet weight in fast 7mms, but my strong pref-

erence in cartridges from 7mm Remington Magnum on up to 7mm STW and 7mm Remington Ultra Mag is for bullets from 160 to 165 grains. In the .280 I kind of split the difference, generally going with 150-grain bullets. Obviously, I have my preferences, but you could use any bullet weight between 140 and 160 grains and never know the difference on game up to elk.

.308

Read my stuff from 30 years ago and you will quickly find that I was a staunch and almost exclusive user of the 180-grain bullet. I still think the 180-grain bullet is by far the most versatile .30 caliber bullet, quite suitable for everything from deer to moose and a sound minimum for big bears. I used to recommend 200-grain bullets for bigger stuff, but with today's better bullets I think 180 grains is plenty in most applications. And for smaller big game such as deer, sheep, goats and the like, today I often use lighter bullets, either 150 grains or 165.

I love the .30-06, and admit grudgingly that the .308 with modern loads is at least 95 percent equal to the .30-06 and generally more accurate. I have used every magnum .30 I can think of, and I've even used the .30-30 quite a bit. This last cartridge, with its lower velocity and tubular-magazine lever actions, is in a different class from all the rest, and my bullet preference can be encapsulated in one word: LEVERevolution.

In the .30-06 I still use 180-grain bullets more than anything else, but for deer-size game these days I'm likely to use the much faster and flatter-shooting 150-grain bullet, and I just might compromise and use 165-grain loads. I had a Remington Model 700 that just loved out-of-the-box Remington 165-grainers, and I used it a great deal. But I've also had fantastic success with 180-grain Nosler Partitions, and in recent years I've taken a lot of game with 180-grain Hornady Interlock Spire Points. The truth is that, at .308 Winchester and .30-06 velocities, you just can't go wrong—and you don't need a bullet that is really hard.

You must be a bit more careful with the fast .30s. You can go with a heavier bullet (180 grains) that's a bit softer, but if you use lighter bullets you need them to be a bit tougher—especially if you need to make a close-range shot or if you're hunting larger game.

The fast .30 I have the most experience with is the .300 Weatherby Magnum, which I've used for three decades with a wide variety of bullets from 150 to 200 grains. In recent years I've pretty much standardized: For deer, sheep and goats I've been using 150-grain Hornady InterBond, fast and vicious, but it holds together; for more general use I go with either a plain old 180-grain Hornady Interlock or a 180-grain Barnes TSX.

On the other hand, my .300 H&H shoots 150-grain Sierra GameKings and 200-grain Sierra GameKings to the same point of impact at 100 yards. I generally used the former for smaller

game and the latter for bigger stuff. A .300 Blaser Magnum I've been using lately just loves 180-grain Barnes TTSX. So with the fast .30s it's another situation where you can't go too far wrong provided you use a bullet tough enough so that it won't come unglued at full velocity.

8mm/.323

I do like the 8mms and honestly believe the larger diameter bullet hits harder, but for me bullet weight depends on the cartridge. I've used the 8mm Remington Magnum quite a lot, the .325 WSM a bit and the 8x57 a very little bit. In the 8x57 you pretty much have to go with lighter bullets, like 180 grains, to get enough velocity to be versatile. The .325 WSM runs into a case capacity issue with heavier bullets, so it's probably at its best with 200-grain slugs.

The 8mm Remington Magnum has plenty of case capacity, and my primary experience with it has been with 220-grain bullets. I've used the 220-grain Sierra GameKing boattail more than anything else. It is not a hard bullet, but with all that weight it has performed wonderfully on game up to elk and eland.

.338

There are light .338 bullets that are pretty good for deer, and there are heavy .338 bullets that would be plenty adequate for Cape buffalo, but I think of the .338 as the perfect elk caliber. It's also just fine for moose and the biggest bears that walk. I find the most useful bullet weights run from 200 to 250 grains. The lighter bullets in this group can be pushed faster and are thus more versatile; the heavier bullets hit harder and penetrate deeper.

It does depend a bit on the cartridge. Milder .33s such as the .338 Federal and .338-06 are probably at their best with 200-grain bullets, again because of case capacity issues.

For years I used 250-grain Noslers almost exclusively in my .338 Winchester Magnum, but they run pretty slow. Today I'd be more likely to compromise and use 225-grain bullets in that cartridge and the .338 RCM.

In the really fast .33s—such as the .340 Weatherby Magnum and the .338 Remington Ultra Mag—I have generally used 250-grain bullets, and the performance on really big game is marvelous. But, man, do these cartridges kick, and the heavy bullets make it worse.

.35

My use of the .35 caliber has been limited to cartridges with moderate velocity, intended and used for short to medium range. Being sort of a heavy-bullet guy, I have most often used 250-grain bullets, including in the .348 (unique bullet diameter of .348 inch) and .358 Winchester, .350 Rigby Rimless and .35 Whelen (all .358-inch bullets).

I'm not prepared to say I've been wrong, but in recent years I've had equally good luck—and flatter trajectories—with 200- and 225-grain bullets. The .35s are, again, needlessly powerful for deer, but they are real thumpers for black bear and both elk and moose in close cover.

Okay, I'm going to stop there. If you're interested in my take on big-bore big game bullets for Africa and such, go online and check out rifleshootermag.com. Just don't forget it's the bullet that really does the job. Choose it wisely.

While the 8mms aren't popular, they make great elk medicine with bullets in the 220-grain neighborhood.

A tougher bullet such as Federal's Trophy Bonded Tip can allow you to cheat a little bit on bullet weight in order to gain a flatter trajectory while not sacrificing anything in the penetration department.

KNOCKOUT PUNCH

KINETIC ENERGY IS ONE WAY TO MEASURE CARTRIDGE PERFORMANCE. TAYLOR'S K. O. VALUES ARE ANOTHER.

by Brad Fitzpatrick

The world of ballistics is often assumed to be black and white. After all, the laws of physics that govern how fast and how far a projectile flies after exiting the muzzle are pretty rigid. Sure, there are outside forces such as wind and barometric pressure that affect the trajectory of a bullet, but the basic rules are firm, and good shooters typically know the vital stats of their favorite cartridge the way sports analysts can rattle off data relating to batting averages and yards per carry.

Yes, we shooters love our numbers, but do we always understand what the numbers are saying? Can statistical loads on cartridges and loads ever give an accurate interpretation of real-world performance?

One of the numbers that most rifle cranks know is the amount of kinetic energy their gun produces. Given in foot-pounds, kinetic energy accounts for a bullet's mass and velocity and uses these numbers to produce a relative figure related to the amount of energy delivered when the bullet strikes.

For years the adage has been that elk require about 2,000 ft.-lbs. of pressure to crumble, and deer require about half that much energy. This is a rough estimate, and no amount of killing power will make up for a lack of shooting ability and bullets in the wrong place, but kinetic energy has always been the most commonly accepted theoretical means of determining a cartridge's capabilities on game.

Kinetic energy values are calculated by multiplying the bullet's weight in grains by the square of the velocity and dividing by 450,400—providing the shooter with a measurable amount of energy, the standard by which most hunters calculate killing power.

In Africa, the legal minimum calibers for killing dangerous game are often given as kinetic energy values, but there are experienced hunters, including many professional hunters, who don't consider kinetic energy as the basis by which to judge whether or not a cartridge is suitable for large and dangerous game.

For instance, the 7mm Shooting Times Westerner and 9.3x62 Mauser both generate about 3,500 ft.-lbs. of energy at the muzzle. Based solely on this criterion, both of these cartridges should be equally adept at killing large and dangerous game such as buffalo and grizzly bear. However, the 9.3x62 is considered an effective dangerous game cartridge (albeit in the low end of the spectrum), and the 7mm STW is not considered suitable by most experts.

The argument for heavier, larger diameter bullets results from the notion that kinetic energy values place too much emphasis on a cartridge's velocity and doesn't take into account the myriad other factors that result in what is deemed "killing power." So if kinetic energy isn't the only factor involved in producing killing power, what other factors should be taken into consideration?

There are many considerations when judging a particular cartridge and load's ability to cleanly kill game. Kinetic energy is certainly one of these considerations, but there are a variety of other factors that determine how a bullet reacts when it actually strikes the target.

To be effective, a bullet must reach its intended target and transfer energy to the animal. This means that the bullet must penetrate in a straight line and perform properly when it reaches the game. Bullet weight, diameter, construction and sectional density (a ratio of the bullet's mass to diameter) are all key factors that affect a bullet's terminal performance.

One man who relied more on practical application than theory with regard to bullet performance was John "Pondoro" Taylor, the legendary African hunter who made a name for himself during the days of the ivory trade. Taylor knew a thing or two about hunting the largest game and is credited with taking more than 1,000 elephants and buffalo, which leaves little doubt to his level of experience and his field experience with heavy animals.

Taylor spent most of his career hunting with rifles that most would consider marginal for professional elephant hunting, namely the .375 H&H, with great success. In his classic work *African Rifles and Cartridges*, Pondoro references what would later become known as Taylor's Knock Out value.

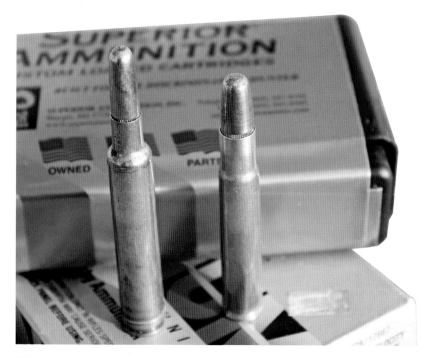

In terms of kinetic energy, the .300 Wby. Mag. (l.) is vastly superior to the .35 Whelen, but according to Pondoro Taylor's calculations the Whelen will do a better job of anchoring a large animal.

Taylor's experience with close-up shooting on large, dangerous game such as elephants led him to develop a formula that he believed was a good predictor of stopping power.

Taylor wasn't interested in kinetic energy as much as he valued what he deemed a "knockout blow," when a bullet killed large and dangerous game cleanly and quickly. He developed his own formula to determine the effectiveness of particular cartridges.

Taylor's formula for KO value is calculated by multiplying bullet diameter, bullet weight (in grains) and velocity together and then dividing by 7,000. In Taylor's formula, high-velocity cartridges aren't given a statistical advantage like they are when calculating kinetic energy.

Incidentally, in his best-known book *Big Game & Big Game Rifles*, Taylor calculated bullet diameter based on nomenclature rather than actual bullet diameter, so he used a value of .400 for the .450/.400 Nitro Express instead of the actual bullet diameter of .405. For the sake of consistency, in the accompanying chart I've used actual bullet diameter instead of traditional nomenclature for evaluation.

Certain bullets, he believed, carried enough energy to simply knock game out, and he believed this transfer of energy was a prod-

uct of bullet weight and diameter as much as it was about sheer velocity. Taylor considered a KO of 40 to be the minimum for really large game such as elephants. The .375 H&H, which Taylor and many other African hunters hold dear, generates a KO value of 40 when firing a 300-grain bullet at 2,550 fps. So loaded, this cartridge develops about 4,300 ft.-lbs. of kinetic energy.

The .404 Jeffery, on the other hand, fires a .423-inch, 400-grain projectile at a modest 2,125 fps. This means the .404 produces 4,010 ft.-lbs. of kinetic energy at

Serious rifle shooters know their numbers—velocities, energies, powder charges and more. KO values are just one more tool they can use to make gun and cartridge choices for a particular hunt.

The days of legal ivory trading have ended, so what value does Taylor's formula have for the average hunter who spends his time pursuing deer, elk, bears and other North American big game? Since kinetic energy values are so widely accepted today as the legitimate measure of a cartridge's capabilities, can we learn anything from Taylor's findings?

Perhaps. Going back to the example of the 7mm STW versus the 9.3x62 Mauser, we can compare kinetic energy values to KO values and, in the process, learn a bit about the personality of these seeemingly disparate cartridges.

With common loads, kinetic energy values for the 7mm STW are only about 7 percent less than for the 9.3x62 (3,590 ft.-lbs. for the former, 3,840 for the latter). This indicates these two cartridges are similar in capability and function. However, the 7mm STW has a KO value of 20.5 while the 9.3x62 has a value of 35.2, a value that is 42 percent higher for the larger cartridge.

This disparity between KO values and kinetic energy becomes more obvious when you com-

pare fast magnums such as the .300 Wby. Mag. with cartridges such as the .35 Whelen that push larger, heavier bullets at lower velocities. The .300 Wby. Mag. drives a 180-grain .308 bullet at about 3,250 fps, and the .35 Whelen pushes a .358-inch, 225-grain projectile at 2,610 fps.

In terms of kinetic energy, the .300 Wby. trounces the .35 Whelen, with the Weatherby producing 4,223 ft.-lbs. of muzzle energy while the Whelen manages only 3,412. This appears to be a decided advantage in favor of the Weatherby, but when you calculate KO

STOPPING POWER

TAYLOR KNOCKOUT VALUE COMPARISON

Cartridge	Bullet Diameter (in.)	Bullet Weight (gr.)	Muzzle Velocity (fps)	Muzzle Energy (ft.-lbs.)	Taylor KO Value
.243 WIN.	.243	90	3,200	2,050	9.9
.270 WSM	.277	130	3,295	3,135	16.9
7MM REM. MAG.	.284	150	3,110	3,221	18.9
.30-06	.308	180	2,700	2,913	21.4
.300 WIN. MAG.	.308	180	3,150	3,975	24.9
.338 FEDERAL	.338	210	3,226	2,630	26.7
.375 H&H MAG.	.375	300	2,550	4,330	41.0

NOTES: Accuracy results are averages of four five-shot groups fired from a rest at 50 yards. Velocities are averages of 20 shots measured 12 feet from muzzle with an Oehler 35P chronograph at an ambient temperature of 90 degrees 1,030 feet above sea level.

values you find that the Whelen has a value of 30 to the .300 Wby.'s 25.8. In Taylor's view, the .35 Whelen was a better cartridge for stopping dangerous game up close than the Weatherby.

The key word is "close." KO values give the shooter an estimate of what the bullet will do at close range and doesn't take into account bullet shape, construction or downrange energy. Because

kinetic energy values favor faster bullets, they don't account for sectional density and bullet diameter and weight. These are all important factors when hunting dangerous game up close like Taylor was.

Neither of these figures takes into account bullet construction and whether or not you hit the vitals, which is ultimately more important than either kinetic energy or KO value.

In truth, Taylor's formula was well-suited for his type of hunting, but for medium-size game at moderate to long ranges kinetic energy still gives a reasonable expectation with regard to a cartridge's capabilities. However, if nothing else, KO value helps us understand that a cartridge's real-world performance on game is a result of a combination of factors.

NORTH AMERICA'S BIG THREE

A THREE-CARTRIDGE BATTERY THAT CAN TACKLE ANYTHING ON THE CONTINENT.

by Craig Boddington

The old saying is "Beware the one-gun man." Many successful hunters not only get by with a single rifle, but also distinguish themselves season after season because they know it and trust it so well. But if you're not a rifle nut you probably aren't reading this magazine. Most of us have multiple rifles, and some of us have dozens. We're not looking for reasons why we should limit ourselves. Also, statistically, the majority of America's 10 million deer hunters never hunt outside their home states or provinces, so they have no genuine need for a robust battery.

But neither extreme is the point of this exercise. Let's just suppose that you're going to hunt North America from top to bottom. We often figure there are 29 varieties of North American big game, although there are more if you get into races and subspecies. Few among us will ever hunt them all; I doubt I'll ever get there. But let's

not worry about that. Instead, figure that you're going to hunt game from small to large and, perhaps more importantly, under a wide variety of conditions.

How many rifles do you really need? I think you need four.

In 40 years of gun writing, this is not the first time I have addressed this subject. But it's been a while, so before you get out pen and paper (or hop on the Internet) to chide me for changing my mind, let me tell you the truth: My tastes and preferences have changed over the years.

Hopefully, we can all agree that it starts with one good .22 rimfire. That's the indispensable tool for training, plinking and small game. Beyond that, I think we can do very nicely with three centerfires: light, medium and heavy. I'll cut the suspense. At this stage in my life, my choices are the .204 Ruger, .270 Win., and .338 Win. Mag. Now I'll try to articulate why.

LIGHT

North America is not blessed with a lot of "small" big game like Africa's pygmy antelope and Europe's roebuck. We do have javelina. In southern Mexico we also have white-lipped peccary and brocket deer, but realistically, these are most commonly hunted with buckshot. On the other hand, serious varminting for non-edible pests such as prairie dogs and ground squirrels is almost uniquely a North American pastime—and we can add in coyotes and bobcats here as well.

To my thinking, in the North American context, the light rifle will be used for non-edible pests under all conditions and for predators up to coyotes, whether called in or sniped. It should also be powerful enough for javelina.

Of my three choices, the .204 Ruger may be the hardest sell. I nix the .17s for three reasons. First, they don't hold up well in the wind; second, coyotes are very tough for their size, and the .17s are questionable for them,

CARTRIDGE	Bullet Weight	Manufacturer/Bullet	Muzzle Velocity (fps)	Muzzle Energy (ft.-lbs.)	100 yd.	Trajectory (in.)* 300 yd.	400 yd.	500 yd.
NORTH AMERICA THREE-CARTRIDGE BATTERY COMPARISONS								
LIGHT								
.204 RUGER	32	Remington AccuTip V	4,225	1,268	0.6	-4.1	-13.1	-28.9
.204 RUGER	40	Hornady V-Max	3,900	1,351	0.7	-4.5	-13.9	-29.7
.223 REM.	40	Winchester Ballistic Silvertip	3,700	1,216	0.1	-5.8	-18.4	-40.9
.223 REM.	50	Black Hills/Hornady V-Max	3,300	1,285	1.3	-6.8	-21.1	-45.6
.22-250 REM.	40	Federal/Nosler Ballistic Tip	4,150	1,530	0.6	-4.2	-13.2	-28.8
.22-250 REM.	50	Hornady V-Max	3,800	1,603	0.8	-5.0	-15.6	-32.8
MEDIUM								
.264 WIN. MAG.	140	Winchester Power-Point	3,030	2,854	1.5	-7.2	-20.8	-42.2
.270 WIN.	130	Federal/Sierra GameKing	3,060	2,702	1.4	-6.5	-19.0	-38.5
.270 WIN.	140	Hornady SST	2,940	2,687	1.4	-6.8	-19.7	-39.7
.270 WIN.	150	Federal/Nosler Partition	2,850	2,705	1.7	-7.5	-21.6	-43.6
.270 WSM	130	Federal/Nosler Ballistic Tip	3,300	3,145	1.1	-5.4	-15.8	-32.2
.270 WSM	140	Norma/Barnes TSX	3,150	3,085	1.2	-5.8	-16.9	-34.0
.270 WSM	150	Winchester Ballistic Silvertip	3,120	3,243	1.3	-5.9	-17.2	-34.7
.270 WBY. MAG.	140	Weatherby/Nosler Ballistic Tip	3,300	3,385	1.1	-5.3	-15.6	-31.5
.270 WBY. MAG.	150	Weatherby/Nosler Partition	3,245	3,507	1.2	-5.5	-16.1	-32.5
.280 REM.	140	Remington Core-Lokt	3,000	2,797	1.5	-7.0	-19.0	-38.4
.280 REM.	150	Federal/Nosler Partition	2,890	2,780	1.7	-7.2	-21.1	-42.5
7MM REM. MAG.	140	Remington Core-Lokt Ultra	3,175	3,133	1.3	-6.1	-18.0	-36.8
7MM REM. MAG.	150	Remington/Swift Scirocco	3,110	3,220	1.3	-5.9	-17.0	-34.0
HEAVY								
.325 WSM	200	Winchester/Nosler AccuBond	2,950	3,866	1.5	-6.8	-19.8	-39.9
8MM REM. MAG.	200	Remington/Swift A-Frame	2,900	3,734	1.8	-8.0	-23.9	-49.6
.338 WIN. MAG.	200	Remington/Nosler Ballistic Tip	2,950	3,866	1.6	-7.1	-20.8	-42.4
.338 WIN. MAG.	225	Hornady InterBond	2,840	4,029	1.7	-7.3	-21.1	-42.3
.338 WIN. MAG.	250	Federal/Nosler Partition	2,660	3,925	2.1	-8.8	-25.2	-50.7
.338 REM. ULTRA MAG	225	Federal/Nosler AccuBond	3,020	4,555	1.4	-6.2	-17.9	-36.0
.338 REM. ULTRA MAG	250	Remington Core-Lokt	2,860	4,540	1.7	-7.6	-22.0	-44.7
.340 WBY. MAG.	200	Weatherby/Nosler Ballistic Tip	3,221	4,607	1.2	-5.8	-17.0	-34.7
.340 WBY. MAG.	225	Weatherby/Hornady InterLock	3,066	4,696	1.2	-6.6	-19.4	-39.6
.340 WBY. MAG.	250	Weatherby/Nosler Partition	2,941	4,801	1.6	-6.9	-20.0	-40.4
.338 LAPUA MAG.	250	Hornady InterLock	2,900	4,668	1.7	-7.3	-21.3	-43.3

*200-yard zero

especially at distance; and third, the .17s are not enough gun for javelina.

Now, honestly, any of the fast .22 centerfires will do, and the most popular choices by far are .223 Rem. and .22-250 Rem. Although it's a newer cartridge and not as popular, I prefer the .204. It is much faster and flatter shooting than the .223. That's in part because of its extremely high velocity (3,900 fps for a 40-grain bullet and up to 4,225 fps for a 32-grain bullet) and in part because .20 caliber bullets are pretty efficient and hold up surprisingly well in the wind.

Its advantage over the .22-250 is less recoil. When shooting small varmints like prairie dogs and ground squirrels, you can call your shots through the scope, which you can't quite do with a .22-250 unless it's a very heavy gun. You can with a .223, but the .204 is a superior varmint cartridge to the .223. And it has plenty of power for game up to coyotes and javelina with the heavier 40-grain bullet.

Note, please, that the .204 is not a deer rifle. With the right bullets the .22 centerfires are, at least in cool hands under the right conditions, but we're discussing a three-rifle battery,

Boddington believes that of today's cartridges, a rifle battery containing these three is capable of taking anything on our continent: (from l.) .204 Ruger, .270 Win., .338 Win. Mag.

so there's no need to have deer in the mix for the light category.

So my vote goes to the .204. I cannot say that it is consistently more accurate than other possibilities, but I can say I have found it to be exceptionally accurate, better on average than the .223 and on par with the .22-250.

MEDIUM

This is the workhorse rifle and cartridge for most North American big game hunting. Its primary use will be deer and other deer-size game, which includes pronghorn, sheep and goat, perhaps on up to caribou.

Clearly, there are dozens of cartridges that would work, but it isn't just about reliably adequate power. You have to look at the full range of conditions and situations. Mule deer in the high country; whitetails in farm country or in thick cover; Coues deer in desert mountains; our four North American sheep in all sorts of mountains; our prairie goat, the pronghorn, on open sagebrush flats; and our real Rocky Mountain goat in nasty cliffs.

We also have to understand that, while hunting North American big game often tends to be somewhat specialized, we don't necessarily pursue western and northern game in a vacuum. So while we can exclude the big bears and aren't trying to select the most perfect setup for elk and moose, our versatile workhorse should at least be elk and moose capable. And since the conditions it's used under will vary tremendously, it must have some reach.

It seems fairly obvious that we're talking about a relatively fast cartridge somewhere between 6.5mm and .30 caliber. I'm going to nix the .30s. I love them, and they have their place, but standard choices,

such as the .308 and .30-06, just don't have the velocity to be ideal in open-country situations.

The numerous magnum .30s certainly do, but I am convinced that you don't need a magnum .30 caliber for hunting North American deer, sheep or goats. This is a departure for me. There was a time when I thought you did need a magnum, and if you're serious about limiting yourself to just one or two rifles for North America, then perhaps you still do. But that's not what we're doing, and I don't have room for a .30 caliber among my three centerfires—not my beloved .30-06, nor my almost as beloved .300 Wby. Mag.

Clearly, the fast .30s work, but their level of recoil is greater than a lot of people are comfortable with. So to mitigate that you have to add gun weight or a blast-producing muzzle brake. But, again, you don't really need a fast .30 in this role, and over time you're going to get tired of explaining why you're using such a big cannon.

So let's take a step down. I think I'm right on the bottom end. For serious versatility you need to start with the fast 6.5mms, which pretty much means the .264 Win. Mag. or perhaps the brand new .26 Nosler. Then you can go on up to the faster 7mms. The .280 Rem. is a fine choice, and there's nothing wrong with the 7mm Rem. Mag. and the numerous other 7mm magnums.

But, although I fought it for many years, I have to admit that Professor O'Connor was right all along. As a young hunter and gun writer, he started with the .270 Win. when it was new in 1925, and he finished with it 52 years later. He figured that neither the .264 Win. Mag. nor the 7mm Rem. Mag. would do anything his beloved .270 wouldn't do.

might actually consider the .270 WSM or .270 Wby. Mag. Study the charts. There's almost nothing in the entire spectrum of hunting cartridges that shoots flatter, yet the recoil is manageable and terminal performance awesome.

I'll stick with the original .270 Win. for three reasons. First, selection of loads. Everybody loads the .270 Win. and with every imaginable .277-inch bullet. Second, selection of rifles. Everybody chambers to the .270 Win. Third, and most important, the .270 Win. gets the job done. It's fast enough, flat enough and powerful enough for any North American deer, sheep or goats—just like Jack O'Connor told us. It's also perfectly adequate for elk, whether close or far. In fact, with the great bullets we have available today, the .270 is probably more adequate for elk than it was in O'Connor's day.

HEAVY

I'm fine hunting elk with the .270. I've used it at close range in timber, and I've used it out at 400 yards and beyond with no problems. But I believe there are better tools for elk, and I know a whole lot more is needed for the biggest bears. Fortunately, we've saved room in our battery for a bigger, more specialized hammer.

The difference in bullet diameter between the 6.5mm and the .270 is just .013 inch; the difference between the .270's .277-inch bullet and the 7mm's .284-inch bullet is even less: .007 inch. The 7mm offers the option of using heavier bullets, but for the class of game this selection is intended for, standard bullet weights of 130 to 150 grains are plenty heavy enough.

There is more than one .270 caliber cartridge, although there aren't nearly as many choices as with other popular bullet diameters. In part I believe this is because the .270 Win. is just plain that good. But the teenage .270 WSM is clearly faster, and Roy Weatherby's .270 Wby. Mag., turning 70 this year, is faster yet.

I have used all three fast .270s quite a bit, and I like all three of them. If your interests or needs shade toward longer ranges and open country, you

There was a time Boddington would've insisted that the fast .30 calibers are best under all conditions for game in the deer class, but these days he's in the .270 Win. camp.

For moose and the largest bears, you can't beat the .338 Win. Mag.'s blend of power, speed and trajectory. Plus, it's a rifle most hunters have no problem handling.

As much as I love the big bores, there is really no place for them in North America. Even the great .375, the versatility king, has extremely limited utility in North America. But we do need a fairly powerful cartridge for the big bears, to include black bears, which certainly can be quite large. And since we have it, it will probably be our primary choice for elk and moose.

I think any of the "fast mediums" are in the running. You can start with the .325 WSM and 8mm Rem. Mag., go up through the .33s, and probably stop at .35 caliber. I love the 8mm Rem. Mag., but it has never been popular and isn't going to be. Mind you, a cartridge doesn't have to be popular to be perfect, but, all things equal, availability matters. For instance, the .358 Norma Mag. would be a fine choice, but it's a rare bird, and both rifles and ammo are scarce. The really fast .33s—the .340 Wby. Mag., .338 Rem. Ultra Mag,

.338 Lapua—are awesome. But they have too much recoil for most of us, whether we admit it or not.

So my vote goes to the .338 Win. Mag. And thus, perhaps uniquely, we can espouse not only Jack O'Connor's favorite, but also invoke the spirit of Elmer Keith. Elmer loved his .33s, and for heavier game he wasn't wrong.

The .338 Win. Mag. was introduced in 1958 in the Winchester Model 70 Alaskan, clearly intended for North America's largest game. Elmer had it right: Load up with a 250-grain bullet, especially the great hunting bullets we have today, and no bear can stand in your way. But he recommended the same heavy-for-caliber bullets for elk and deer, and with the bullets we have today this isn't necessary. Lighter bullets can be pushed a lot faster, reducing recoil and stretching trajectory.

With Elmer's heavy bullets the .338 is devastatingly effective, but it's slow. Cut down the bullet weight and it shoots flat enough for anything most of us need to do. With aerodynamic 200- or 225-grain bullets the .338 becomes, in my view, your arm of choice for elk and moose, and thus the right choice for combo hunts involving larger game.

As the chart suggests, you can get all the range you really need. And if you're one of today's long-range advocates, then here's an irrefutable truth: At long range, when bullet performance can no longer be relied upon, frontal area does make a difference.

So, you have my choices: .204 Ruger, .270 Win. and .338 Win. Mag. It's a fun exercise, and there are no right or wrong answers. These are not the same three I might have cited 20 years ago, so it will be interesting to see if I feel the same way in another 20 years.

THE TRUTH ABOUT EFFICIENCY

THE TERM GETS BANDIED ABOUT IN TODAY'S WORLD OF CARTRIDGES, BUT IT'S NOT AS STRAIGHTFORWARD AS YOU MIGHT IMAGINE.

by Brad Fitzpatrick

Ballisticians and rifle cranks love the word "efficiency," and it's become a common part of our vernacular. We love a specific rifle cartridge because it's so efficient. We purchase a rifle chambered for a new round because it's more efficient than what we were hunting with last year. The term has become a sales pitch for cartridges in much the same way that the term "reliability" sells new cars, but how well do we understand the concept of cartridge efficiency—and how does it relate to energy, trajectory, pressure and a host of other interconnected factors that come into play every time we punch a primer?

Efficiency is a tricky subject, and when labeling a cartridge as "efficient," we must remember that there are a number of factors that can affect overall cartridge efficiency. Most shooters know certain cartridges work better with certain powders. This seems simple enough, but some shooters give credit to a cartridge for the work of the propellant.

When ammunition companies switched from blackpowder to smokeless propellants, the velocity and energy produced by the .30-30 Win. jumped dramatically. Was the .30-30 suddenly a more potent cartridge? You bet it was, but switching powders accomplished this rise in velocity and energy. Likewise, Hornady's Superformance ammunition is considerably faster than most traditional factory ammo, but that's a result of Hornady's use of a proprietary powder. They didn't change the .30-06; they just gave it a boost.

This may seem like basic information, but discussions on efficiency can sometimes turn into a bad sketch comedy where misconceptions and misinformation leave everyone confused and discombobulated. First, and this is important, efficiency is relative to propellant. What works in one round may not work for another. That's important to understand. Forty grains of IMR 4350 doesn't burn at the same rate that 40 grains of Reloder 25 does, so it's important to keep things relative.

Like with any good science experiment, we have to keep the variables the same. It won't do us any good to compare the .243 Win.'s ability to push an 80-grain bullet at 3,000 fps in front of 46 grains of IMR 7828 with the .300

Wby. Mag.'s capacity to launch a 150-grain bullet at 3,363 fps with 86 grains of Reloder 22. That'd be like saying a Rolls Royce jet engine is more efficient than a Briggs and Stratton because it can fly a jet to Switzerland. Power alone doesn't equate to efficiency.

We must also take into account variables such as burn rate. Load a hot, long-cased magnum with a powder that burns too fast and you're never going to see the results you could achieve with a slower-burning propellant. Propellant choice is variable, and good handloaders understand that they have to match the

cartridge with the right powder to effectively compare efficiency.

The one variable that remains constant is the design of the case.

The standardized case for a .30-06 has retained exactly the same dimensions for the last hundred-odd years, and the primary factor behind how "efficient" a cartridge is boils down to one thing: case architecture. To understand efficiency, you truly must have a handle on how rifles cases are designed and how changes to a design will alter things such as burn rate and compression. Interior dimensions, the slope of the shoulder, the overall length and other factors play into overall powder column burn. Case design and efficiency go hand-in-hand—period.

It's generally assumed that, with all things being equal, a larger case capacity reduces overall efficiency. Take a look at the accompanying chart where I have matched several 7mm loads and their efficiency with each load in feet per second per grain of powder—one way to measure efficiency. Case capacity gets larger as you go down the list. Consequently, velocity goes up (as does energy) but efficiency drops in every case.

Generally speaking, larger cases allow for more powder to be stuffed in the load, but overall efficiency goes down. The 7mm WSM and the 7mm Rem. Mag. are a particularly interesting comparison, because while they are very close in overall case capacity (the 7mm WSM holds 83.0 grains of water, the 7mm Rem. Mag. holds 83.2), the 7mm WSM

One of the most dramatic examples of efficiency differences based on case design is found is the .30 T/C (l.) versus the .30-06. Even though it's much smaller, the T/C round nearly matches '06 velocities with similar weight bullets.

The 7mm Rem. Mag. case (r.) will hold more powder and push a bullet faster, but it is less efficient than the .280 Ackley. You have to ask whether the boost you usually get from bigger cases is worth the price in recoil.

offers a 1 percent increase in efficiency. The similarity in overall case capacity indicates that it is the overall design of the Winchester's case that leads to efficiency.

I ran these comparisons with a couple different powders, and while, as I mentioned, it's true you could tweak the efficiency of a particular cartridge by matching it up with a particular powder, on an apple-to-apple basis the cartridges with smaller volumes are more efficient.

Winchester's line of Short Magnums (and Super Short Magnums, which have faded away) was designed with efficiency in mind. I contacted Mike Stock, centerfire product manager at Winchester ammunition, and asked him how the case design of the WSMs achieves this increase. According to Stock, the WSM's case diameter and short overall length result in a more efficient overall burn of the powder, meaning that more

powder is burned more quickly. This means that there is very little powder that is left unburned, and this allows the WSM cartridges to achieve maximum velocity in shorter barrels.

"Improved airflow efficiency and a large diameter powder column make these cartridges more efficient," Stock said. "A short, fat powder column is so near the primer that you are getting more burn before the bullet leaves the case."

But Stock said a major factor in the efficiency of current cartridges such as the WSMs is at least also due in part to having more powders from which to choose.

"When the .30-06 was designed there were only a few powder options," he said. "Today, there are 30 or 40 more, which allows engineers to match new cartridges with the proper propellant."

According to Stock, magnum cartridges "belch a lot of unburnt powder" in short barrels. Mod-

ern, more efficient loads allow for maximum velocity from shorter tubes, all while staying within pressure limits. From a real-world standpoint, that means hunters can carry a rifle that is lighter and has a shorter barrel and can expect the same results they could only achieve with heavier guns with long pipes only a few years ago. Better efficiency also means cartridges can almost match the trajectory of older magnums with less muzzle blast, recoil and powder.

"You can change powders, bullets and barrel length, but there's nothing you can do to change case volume on a particular cartridge," Stock said. "Modern cartridges are designed around modern powders."

These realizations have led to a change in overall cartridge design during recent years, and if you examine new cartridge designs (the WSMs, Ruger's Compact Magnums, the 6.5 Creedmoor and others), there has been a shift

Better efficiency doesn't directly translate into better accuracy, but more efficient rounds tend to get their jobs done with less recoil and muzzle blast—which usually means you'll shoot them better.

7MM EFFICIENCIES

Cartridge	Bullet Weight (gr.)	Powder Charge (gr.)	Muzzle Velocity (fps)	Velocity Per Grain of Powder (fps)
7mm-08 Rem.	160	44.0	2,650	66.2
.280 Rem.	160	50.5	2,810	55.6
.280 Ackley Improved	160	53.7	2,813	52.4
7mm WSM	160	57.5	2,894	50.3
7mm Rem. Mag.	160	60.0	2,998	50.0

NOTES: All data generated with IMR 4350

in cartridge architecture toward wider, straight-walled cases with sharper shoulders and minimal body taper. That's no accident; it is a direct effort toward getting more out of shorter, more efficient cartridges.

The current upswing in long-range shooting and hunting (regardless of what you think of the latter) means more rifle owners are stretching the limits of their guns, and according to Stock, efficiency should be a concern to long-range shooters. At extreme ranges, bullet design is very important, and bullets with a high ballistic coefficient buck the wind better and lose velocity more slowly than bullets with low BCs. But serious long-range shooters need to understand why efficiency is critical because the endeavor requires that you are getting the most out of every grain of powder you're burning.

According to Dave Emary, chief ballistician at Hornady, understanding how case design and propellants affect a cartridge is critical to selecting the right cartridge. Newer powders offer hunters and

shooters options when developing loads, for instance, and improving efficiency should be a consideration for any reloader.

"Basically, efficiency is getting the most push you can for the money," Emary said. He says that over-bored cartridges (high powder capacity with a small bore diameter) tend to produce more recoil, more muzzle blast and require longer barrels and slower-burning powders to work effectively.

"More efficient cartridges are typically more accurate because there is less bullet tip-off when the projectile exits the muzzle, and they are more shootable because there is less recoil and muzzle blast. In addition, high velocity bullets reduce barrel life."

For comparison, he points to the .308 Win. versus the .30-06 Springfield. With bullets up to about 165 grains, the .308 delivers similar velocities with five to seven grains less powder. The advantage of a larger case is that it works better with heavier bullets. Over-bored cartridges shooting lighter bullets are inefficient, and he pointed to

the example of the .264 Win. Mag. versus the 6.5 Creedmoor. The larger .264 Win. Mag. requires a long barrel and careful powder selection and produces higher muzzle energy. In addition, lighter calibers are more shootable and are less likely to spew unburnt (read: wasted) powder from the muzzle.

According to Nosler reloading data, the 6.5 Creedmoor will drive a 140-grain .264-inch bullet at 2,672 fps when using a max load of W760 powder. The .264 Win. Mag., using the same bullet and 54.5 grains of the same powder (also a max load), achieves a muzzle velocity of 2,942 fps. The 6.5 Creedmoor is averaging just under 66 fps per grain of powder while the .264 Win. Mag. is making just under 54 fps with a grain of powder. The .264 Win. Mag. load requires 25 percent more powder to achieve a nine percent increase in velocity over the Creedmoor, and the .264 Win. Mag. requires a longer, heavier barrel to do so.

"Everybody thinks about speed, but that's not the only consideration," Emary said. "A .300 Win.

Mag. firing a 150-grain bullet is an extremely inefficient cartridge and is less shootable than smaller rounds."

Understanding efficiency and cartridge design is important for hunters. In any hunting situation you are faced with multiple variables that, when combined, result in the success or failure of a particular shot on game—given that the bullet is correctly placed. Many of these we know and understand; bullet design, shot angle, recoil and muzzle blast (and our ability to handle these without flinching), velocity and even gun weight are critical factors when you are selecting the right gun/load combination for your next hunt. Efficiency plays a role as well.

For most big game hunting at moderate ranges, the efficiency of a cartridge plays a greater role in the result of the hunt than you might initially assume. The 7mm Rem. Mag. is a great deer cartridge, but you aren't getting as much bang for your buck as you might think. The cartridge's larger case capacity means that it is

capable of firing a projectile much faster than a smaller, more efficient cartridge such as the 7mm-08 Rem. But that extra power comes at a price, and because it is more efficient, the smaller 7mm-08 has a trajectory curve that is very close to the magnum out to 200 yards, and it can be built on smaller, lighter rifles that kick less and cost less to shoot.

Mountain hunters should be particularly interested in efficiency, too. When you are climbing and hiking at high elevation, every ounce you carry matters, so you'd better be sure that you aren't carrying any wasted weight. Smaller, more efficient rounds like the 7mm WSM allow you to achieve virtually the same trajectory you would glean from a 7mm Rem. Mag. or Wby. Mag. with a longer case, but they will work on short-action rifles with shorter barrels.

Even dangerous game rifles are benefitting from the new age of more efficient cartridges. Take the .375 Ruger, which was designed by Hornady. Its shorter, fatter case is more efficient than

the long, sloping case of the .375 H&H and can be built on rifles with a standard .30-06-length action. A shorter action means a shorter bolt stroke, and shorter bolt stroke means faster follow-up shots. Ruger and Hornady accomplished this by creating a cartridge that had the same base diameter as the .375 H&H (.532 inch) but had a wider, straighter powder column and a sharper shoulder that increased capacity and efficiency. The result was a short .375 that was more efficient and more powerful than the original.

That's not to say that cartridges like the 7mm Rem. Mag. or the .375 H&H are obsolete. In fact, they're both great choices. Efficiency perhaps isn't the most important consideration when selecting a cartridge, but it is an essential element of cartridge design that is worth bearing in mind when you select a rifle. If you can accomplish what you need with less powder, less recoil and a lighter rifle, isn't that an option worth considering?

FOOT-POUND FALLACY

by Craig Boddington

ENERGY PLAYS A ROLE IN CARTRIDGE EFFECTIVENESS, BUT HOW IT'S TRANSFERRED MEANS MORE THAN MERE NUMBERS.

Decades have passed since Col. Townsend Whelen theorized we should have 1,000 ft.-lbs. of energy at the animal to cleanly take deer-size game. This isn't a bad rule of thumb because kinetic energy expressed in foot-pounds is a proven scientific formula: The amount of force required to move one pound one foot.

I have always agreed with Whelen, but not for the obvious reasons. The 1,000 ft.-lbs. standard is not guaranteed to flatten a deer, but provided other factors (like adequate bullet construction) are present, this level of kinetic energy is required to get the bullet into the vitals. And, ultimately, adequate penetration into life-essential organs is the only way to kill game.

Whelen's rule was for deer-size game. Others, me included, have gone further and suggested 2,000 ft.-lbs. at the animal provides a sound minimum for elk, and for 100 years we have established something between 4,000 and 5,000 ft.-lbs. as a sensible minimum for the world's largest game.

Several alternative methods have been promulgated. Some of them are useful for comparison, but none is

quite as scientific as kinetic energy expressed in foot-pounds. Elmer Keith worked the opposite, "pounds-feet" or momentum, which may have some value. John "Pondoro" Taylor's theory of "knock-out value" included little science but did take into account bullet frontal area. Still touted occasionally, his KO value actually has utility in comparing one cartridge to anoth-

er, but its failure for today's hunter is that it was intended to compare solid, non-expanding bullets and not the bullet designs commonly used now.

How then are we supposed to view energy? Think about it this way. Which is likely to affect you the most: taking a hammer blow just below the sternum or being stabbed with a knitting needle in the same place? The knitting needle is more likely to be fatal, given some time, but the hammer is going to have a much more physical impact on you initially. This is because the hammer develops more kinetic energy, all of which is transferred upon impact.

To my knowledge, we have not found a way to properly evaluate, let alone measure, the transfer of kinetic energy from a projectile to a living target. We do know a surface wound is messy and painful, but, absent infection, not necessarily fatal. We also know perforation of the heart or both lungs is generally fatal, but all experienced hunters have seen heart- or lung-shot animals go for some distance while others drop in their tracks to similar shots.

The whole thing is complicated by the fact that no two living creatures react in exactly the same way upon receipt of a bullet. But while sheer kinetic energy as a number probably isn't as important as we make it, I do think we're missing something vital in not really understanding how much and how quickly energy is transferred.

There are two basic schools of bullet performance: Those who prefer complete penetration and those who want all of the bullet's energy expended in the animal. The latter group is probably also divided into those who like to find their beautifully mushroomed bullets against the skin on the far side and those who are perfectly happy if the bullet goes to pieces as long as it first penetrates into the vitals.

There is a sound rationale for an energy level offering complete penetration in that the resulting exit wound offers better blood trails, and if we're faced with problematic shot angles we can probably count on sufficient penetration. I'm not aware of any testing designed to measure veloc-

ities of bullets exiting from targets that simulate game animals, but you have to assume retained energy for any exiting bullet—energy not expended in the animal.

The "stay in the animal" school of thought is an extremely valid argument. Whatever kinetic energy the bullet had was expended inside the animal, regardless of whether the bullet fragmented in the vitals or lodged or against the hide on the far side.

But here is where it gets tricky. If energy transfer from bullet to animal tissue is important—and I believe it is—is there any way to measure it?

Let's look at four scenarios. Bullets A, B, C and D hit the shoulder of a deer with 1,000 ft.-lbs. of remaining energy. Bullet A expands prematurely. It blows up, creating a nasty surface wound only an inch deep. Bullet B also blows up, but it makes it into the chest cavity, with penetration of about nine inches. Bullet C is found against the hide on the far side. (This is a mid-size deer, so penetration is about 15 inches.) Bullet D exits, center punches a sapling on the far side and exits even that.

Bullet A just plain failed, but it transferred all of its energy on impact. The deer may well have been knocked flat by the sheer impact but also may have gotten up and run off. Bullet B didn't exactly fail (depending on what you wanted), but aside from fragmentation, it expended all of its energy during nine inches of penetration. Bullet C held together and fully expended its energy during 15 inches of penetration. It came to rest on the far side because it lacked the energy to penetrate the skin a second time.

You see what I'm getting at? Bullet D did what a lot of folks want their bullets to do, but after exiting the animal it still had enough velocity and energy to penetrate a tree, which does the hunter no good at all. It penetrated well, but clearly expended only a portion of its energy within the animal. If you are of the school desiring through-and-through penetration, you have to accept that bullet energy will be wasted.

Is this bad? Not necessarily. You must decide which bullet performance pleases you and gives you the most confidence.

For sure, overpenetration is better than lack of penetration. In my example, Bullet A is pure trouble, but Bullet D is fine if it's what you want—and I did want that for many years. Today, however, I'm okay with Bullet B on deer-size game, and I'll take Bullet C across the board. Exit wounds do leak a bit more and expedite tracking, but over the years I have become more convinced I do less tracking when the bullet stays in the animal and expends all of its energy.

We know bullet shape is critical to ballistic coefficient, which is essentially a comparative measure of a bullet's ability to retain velocity. It is not so widely known that bullet shape also affects energy transfer, and, unfortunately, we can't have it both ways. Sharply pointed bullets are aerodynamic and have higher BCs, but they're the knitting needle from my earlier comparison. Blunt-nose bullets lose velocity more quickly and have a more arcing trajectory, but they are the hammer.

Today most of us shoot spitzer bullets as a matter of course, but if you have any experience with roundnose bullets, you probably know they seem to deal a noticeably heavier initial blow than a spitzer at equal velocity. And in my experience, flat-point bullets hit even harder. I believe we are seeing energy transfer in action.

Obviously, penetration to (or through) the vitals remains essential, but I believe initial energy transfer of traditional blunt-nose bullets is why the good old .30-30 kills deer the way it does despite unimpressive ballistics. And big woods hunters who want to drop deer in their tracks often rely on archaic "brush-busters" such as the .35 Rem., .444 Marlin and .45-70. None of these produce as much kinetic energy as, say, a .270, but they flatten game with authority. Part of it is bullet frontal area, and another part is the blunt-nosed bullet—both of which contribute to a rapid initial energy transfer.

Within the large spectrum of expanding bullets, we simply must take into account bullet design: how much and how quickly they expand. The amount of expansion ultimately determines penetration. The more the bullet expands, the more resistance it meets. Velocity is also a factor because it enables the bullet to overcome resistance, but velocity is also a great enemy to consistent bullet performance. For instance, most .30 caliber bullets perform well at .308 and .30-06 velocities, but some become unreliable bombs in faster .30 caliber magnums.

Regardless of velocity, however, hunters who desire through-and-through penetration gravitate to tougher bullets that hold together

---

VELOCITY IS ALSO A GREAT ENEMY TO CONSISTENT BULLET PERFORMANCE.

---

well and don't expand a huge amount. Good examples range from the great Nosler Partition to today's homogeneous-alloy expanding bullets.

Hunters who like to find beautifully mushroomed bullets "against the hide on the far side" are likely to choose bonded-core bullets. Expansion tends to be radical, as much as twice original diameter, but core bonding keeps the bullet together, and weight enhances penetration.

Hunters who want maximum damage to the vitals without undue concern about what the recovered bullet looks like—or exactly where it comes to rest provided it gets to the vitals and dispatches the animal quickly—probably have the widest spectrum of bullets to choose from. Traditional cup-and-core bullets still perform well. Lead-core, polymer-tipped, non-bonded bullets are volatile but often work like lightning striking on deer-size game.

Now we're getting into how quickly the bullet expands. I think this has a lot to do with energy transfer. Regardless of how much they ultimately expand—or how deeply they penetrate—round-nose and flat-point bullets tend to deal the heavy initial blow I spoke of. Polymer-tipped bullets tend to expand quickly because, upon impact, the polymer tip is driven down into the bullet to initiate expansion.

Hollowpoint bullets also tend to expand quickly, and I believe rapid expansion also applies to the homogeneous-alloy bullets. Years ago, when

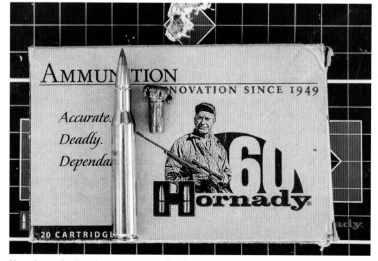

How dramatically a homogeneous-alloy bullet such as the GMX expands is dependent on its cavity design and impact velocity. After expansion is achieved, they behave much like solids, holding together and penetrating deeply.

the Barnes X was new, I did a couple of cull hunts in Australia. Although expansion is limited in this type of bullet (which today includes Hornady GMX, Barnes TSX and TSSX, Federal Trophy Copper, Nosler E-Tip and more) and penetration is extreme, it seemed then—and still appears—this style delivers a noticeably heavy initial blow out of proportion to the actual expansion.

Whether tipped or not, these bullets are all essentially hollowpoints, with a nose cavity that limits the amount of expansion. My theory is these hollowpoints accomplish their

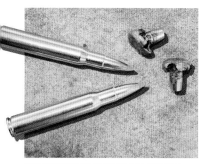

Bonded bullets such as the Federal Trophy Bonded Tip produce the classic huge mushroom and maximum energy transfer, but because the core and jacket are bonded, they tend to retain more weight for better penetration.

expansion quickly due to their nose cavity and then behave essentially as solids, holding together and continuing to penetrate. These bullets are not everyone's cup of tea because expansion is not radical, and few will be recovered. But they do deliver a heavy initial blow, and on solid tissue, such as a shoulder, you can often hear this in the solid crack of the bullet hitting. I believe this is energy transfer.

It is easy to obtain comparative measures of penetration, and recovered bullets can be measured for expansion and weighed for weight retention. It is difficult, perhaps impossible, to scientifically evaluate this business of energy transfer. I do believe it's real, and we can certainly see it in action by shooting water bottles and melons. Measuring it? I don't have a clue, but last year, at the Bisley range in England, I saw a demonstration that got me thinking.

Traditional bullet testing is done in ballistic gelatin or packed wet newspapers. These media show penetration depth but not how quickly a bullet expands or what kind of wound cavity it produces—factors I believe to be key elements in energy transfer. The test I witnessed in England used ballistic soap, which retains an intact wound channel. It was conducted by

a Hornady representative and compared only the company's InterBond, InterLock, GMX and SST (all 150 grains in .308 Win.).

No wider comparison is suggested, and it is accepted this was just a simple demonstration, not a definitive test. But it was interesting nonetheless.

Predictably, the fast-opening SST showed the most distortion, the least recovered weight and the largest cavity diameter: an explosive 4.8 inches. Also predictably, the recovered homogeneous-alloy GMX expanded less than its brethren, retained the most weight (99 percent) and achieved the deepest penetration.

Because the GMX expanded less, its cavity was the smallest at 3.88 inches in diameter, but the distance from entry to maximum cavity diameter was the shortest—just four inches. The difference was not dramatic, but it does seem to confirm my theory that this type of homogeneous-alloy bullet, though more limited in expansion than most lead-core bullets, does its expansion more quickly, perhaps transferring more energy in a shorter distance. Depending on what you want, this does not make it the most perfect bullet. Total penetration was 19.4 inches, meaning it would most likely exit deer-size game.

Second in penetration among these bullets was the InterBond at 16.4 inches, meaning it might exit a deer, depending on shot angle and placement and the size of the deer. The InterLock and SST were equal in penetration at 14.8 inches, which suggests these particular bullets could have been "against the hide on the far side."

The obvious problem with this and most testing media is their uniformity. They can't accurately replicate bones and tissue layers of varying densities, all of which change with shot angle and animal size. So, to me, this business of how and when a bullet's kinetic energy is transferred into game animals—and what effect it has—remains unknown. There may not be any definitive way to solve the mystery, but I'm convinced there is much more to it than the sheer number of foot-pounds.

Unlike other test media, ballistic soap provides a lasting (and measurable) picture of terminal bullet performance. The large initial wound cavity seems to represent the speed and violence of bullet expansion, which Boddington believes is related to energy transfer

STEPPING DOWN

by Craig Boddington

STOP TAKING A BEAT-
ING! THERE ARE LOTS OF
CAPABLE CARTRIDGES
THAT WON'T KICK YOU
INTO NEXT WEEK.

I discovered the writings of Robert Ruark as an impressionable teen-ager, shortly before his death in 1965. I devoured his posthumous collection, *Use Enough Gun*, and I took his advice to heart and always went the more powerful route when choosing a rifle cartridge. It wasn't entirely Ruark's fault. In the postwar years, a young zealot named Roy Weatherby preached the gospel of velocity and proved extremely adept at making headlines in the sporting press of the day—kicking off what I call the First Magnum Craze, which started in the late 1950s. For the next decade virtually every new cartridge wore a belt, carried a magnum suffix and promised more velocity, more energy and more performance than anything that had gone before.

These promises weren't altogether true. In those innocent pre-chrono-graph days, there was the occasion-al glimmer of blue sky in published figures, and little details such as over-bore capacity were ignored. Many of us believed the hype, and we bought into it. Even Jack O'Connor, already the most popular and influential gun writer who ever lived, couldn't stem the tide. His was like a small voice

in the wilderness when, in 1958, he opined that the hot, new .264 Win. Mag. couldn't do anything his beloved .270 could not do; a few years later he said the same thing about the 7mm Rem. Mag. Of course, O'Connor was exactly right.

Many years passed before I grudgingly accepted that wisdom. Like so many youngsters, I started hunting with a .243 Win., but by the mid-'60s

I had a .264 Win. Mag. and thought it was magic. I had a .375 H&H before I was 20, and it accounted for my first elk, my first sheep, my first moose and so forth.

In the early 1980s most of my guns were stolen, and for a time the only firearms I owned were a well-worn Model 12 skeet gun and a left-hand Weatherby Mark V in .300 Wby. Mag. I used that big Weatherby for everything for a couple of seasons. Later, I bought a Remington M700 in 7mm Rem. Mag. and a pre-'64 Model 70 .375, and both of those rifles saw a lot of service over the next few years. And since I did a lot of my early writing during that time, it's no surprise people consider me a magnum maniac.

The adage to "use enough gun" suggests there must also be such things as too much and too little. I do believe there are minimal requirements for our various classes of big game: Elk require more power and penetration than deer, and big bears and buffalo require even more of what my old friend Charlie Askins called "muzzle swoosh."

Perhaps also implied in the "enough gun" admonition is there might be something out there "just right" for certain purposes. Maybe there is, but this seems an elusive formula. It appears to me there is almost always a bunch of cartridges that will work just fine for a given sporting purpose. We can all pick our favorites and make our campfire arguments, and we can also increase performance by choice of bullet. But, realistically, there are broad ranges of suitability, and the hairs we like to split are actually pretty fine.

For instance, given a reasonably suitable choice of bullet, I doubt there are many game animals that will notice the difference between a 6.5mm, a .270 and a 7mm. Given a bit of velocity and a decent bullet, all three calibers can certainly be used for game up to elk. I might argue that a .30 caliber is better for elk (because I think it is), but the window of suitability is wide, so an error has to be pretty gross before finger-pointing starts. The 6mms and .25s are unquestionably marginal for elk, but you need to go on up to the big bears before you can say one is foolishly under-gunned in choosing them.

"Over-gunned" is perhaps even more difficult to pin down. In Africa the .375 H&H is often used as a one-rifle safari battery. Too much gun for small antelope? Sure, but it works and keeps on working throughout the spectrum. If, instead, one chose a .458 Lott, then one might be better armed for the larger stuff, but on the smaller plains game there might not be enough ranging ability and certainly no reason to get kicked into next week on a daily basis.

Obviously, velocity makes a difference, not only in trajectory but also in terminal energy, but I strongly believe a .30 caliber hits harder than a 6.5, .270 or 7mm. I also believe a magnum .30 offers some of the greatest flexibility across our entire spectrum of calibers and cartridges.

I don't consider the .30-06 a big gun, but many people do. It is worth remembering that America's darling .30-06 is actually the most powerful cartridge ever adopted as standard issue by a military power. During its long tenure as our service cartridge, the .30-06, in both Springfield and Garand, was revered for its battlefield performance, but recruits lacking previous shooting experience told horror stories of bruised shoulders and uncontrollable flinches.

The .30-06 is a powerful cartridge. It is too much gun for youngsters and people of smaller stature—and too much gun for any beginner. Well, what about the .308? Yes, it has a bit less recoil than the .30-06, but it's usually built into lighter rifles, which increase recoil. The .308 is also too much gun for a lot of people.

The problem with recoil is we all have different thresholds, and you really don't know how much is too much until you go well beyond what is comfortable. Once you cross that bridge, you will be immediately aware, but the damage may already be done. The most normal physiological reaction to too much recoil is a flinch, which is easy to get but very hard to cure. The only way I know to cure a rifle-shooting flinch is to go back to the basics and start over with several bricks of non-recoiling .22 rimfire. But that's not going to bring down your next big game animal. And even if flinching isn't your problem per se, many people as they age simply find shooting rifles with significant amounts of recoil—and here I count the .30-06 as I mentioned earlier—to be a less-than-pleasant experience.

Younger, smaller and newer shooters have the same problem. And if we're not enjoying ourselves, we're missing out on what hunting's all about.

There are ways to mitigate recoil. The easiest is probably gun weight, but in the field you have to carry that

You can mitigate recoil with kick-reducing rifle rests or with muzzle brakes. Or you can simply decide to switch to a cartridge generating less recoil.

Beginners and younger shooters simply can't handle cartridges such as the .30-06, and as we age, a lot of us can't, either. That's why rounds like the 7mm-08 make more sense for deer-size game

weight. On the range, I customarily use a Caldwell Lead Sled, a wonderful device that, in effect, adds 25 or 50 pounds of weight to the rifle and makes a pussycat out of almost anything.

Muzzle brakes are also extremely effective, but they're noisy—especially for bystanders. Hunting partners and guides hate them, and I'm already deaf enough, so I prefer not to use them.

There is another option: Understanding the broad range of suitability for most classes of game, think about downsizing. Especially with today's wonderful hunting bullets, I don't use the .33s nearly as much as I used to. There aren't many things you can't do with a .30 caliber and a good 180-grain bullet, and even the faster .30s kick a whole lot less than a .33 with a 250-grain bullet.

But most of us only occasionally must make a conscious choice between a .30 caliber and a .338, and here in North America, such a decision is typically limited to elk, bears and moose.

The question becomes, how much gun do you really need for the big game most of us hunt most of the time? And here we're talking primarily about deer, of course. My friend and editor, Scott Rupp, loves the .25s, and indeed there is almost no deer hunting you can't do with a .25-06 or, for that matter, a mild-mannered .257 Roberts.

I do not love the .25s. Instead, I prefer the 6.5s: old-timers like the 6.5x55, brash newcomers like the .260 Rem. and 6.5 Creedmoor. And I still have a soft spot for the faster .264 Win. Mag., lots of performance and relatively little recoil, although I will admit it's not exactly a popular choice due to limited rifles and ammunition—and it's also not exactly "stepping down."

When Rupp needs a bigger gun than the .25-06, the .280 Rem. is one of his favorites. Though more of a cult cartridge than a top seller, the .280 could well be the best cartridge based on the .30-06 case. I've used it now and again, most recently to flatten a big-bodied Kansas whitetail, but it's not one of my personal favorites. Again, no real reason. Further, as Rupp will tell you, because it's based on the '06 case, the .280 is not a big step down in terms of recoil—except that it generally employs lighter bullets than its .30 caliber parent, with the 140-grain bullet the most prevalent.

Instead, I'm a big fan of the old 7x57 Mauser and the newer 7mm-08 Rem. The former has nostalgia and class; the latter offers incredible performance and is an ideal choice for beginning hunters. While the 7x57 is my "go-to" whitetail cartridge, I've outfitted both daughters with 7mm-08s.

And then, of course, we have to get back to Professor O'Connor, who was right all along. His beloved .270 is hard to beat. When I was a beginning writer, O'Connor was still active, so I couldn't be so brash as to attempt to write about his cartridge, but even at the height of my magnum phase, I always had a .270, and I have used the cartridge a great deal.

My wife, Donna, has taken the vast majority of her game with a .270, and for me, it has worked perfectly on game up to elk. Bullet weight is a significant factor in recoil. The .270 with a 130-grain bullet is mild-mannered, and with the bullets we have today, it's even more effective than in O'Connor's time. And although the point of this story is stepping down, I do recommend the .270 WSM when you need a flat-shooting rifle. It has amazing performance with surprisingly little recoil.

It's also possible to downsize even more. I started hunting, with a Model 70 .243, and for years one of my favorite combo varmint/deer rifles was a Ruger No. 1 in .243. As a big game cartridge the .243 is not a long-range number, but for stalking pronghorns and a whole lot of deer hunting it's deadly—partly because it's plenty powerful enough, and partly because it's so easy to shoot well.

Just this year I realized that it's been awhile since I've owned a .243, so I bought a Ruger American .243 in the new left-hand action. Maybe even I'm downsizing.

STEP-DOWN POSSIBILITIES

If you're ready to stop taking a beating, you have a lot of choices to step down in recoil. I selected common bullet weights for cartridges mentioned in Boddington's article and averaged 200-yard energy figures for loads you're likely to find on a dealer's shelf—except the Creedmoor, figures for which are based on a single load. I chose 200 yards because most shots occur at that distance or less. Conventional wisdom says it requires 2,000 ft.-lbs. of energy to cleanly take elk-size game, 1,000 ft.-lbs. to cleanly take deer-size game—given proper bullet choice, of course. Cartridges are ranked by energy in descending order. Relative Recoil Factors, from Bob Forker's *Ammo & Ballistics 5* book, can help you determine what kind of recoil reduction you might expect from a rifle you currently shoot to one you're thinking of downsizing to. Just keep in mind these figures—derived from muzzle momentum of the bullet and expelled powder gas for a typical loading—don't necessarily match the bullet weights I used in the chart and that gun/scope weight plays a big role in felt recoil. Relative Recoil Factors are just another piece of information to consider.
—*J. Scott Rupp*

STEP-DOWN POSSIBILITIES			
Cartridge	Bullet Weight (gr.)	200-Yard Energy (ft.-lbs.)	Recoil Factor
.338 WIN. MAG.	250	2,950	2.93
.300 WIN. MAG.	180	2,675	2.39
7MM REM. MAG.	140	2,280	2.06
.270 WSM	130	2,250	2.00
.30-06	180	2,140	2.19
.280 REM.	140	2,080	1.95
.264 WIN. MAG.	140	2,030	1.91
.270 WIN.	130	1,985	1.82
.308 WIN.	150	1,890	1.95
6.5 CREEDMOOR	129	1,890	1.73
7MM-08 REM.	140	1,785	1.80
.25-06 REM.	117	1,720	1.57
.260 REM.	140	1,700	1.73
7x57 MAUSER	140	1,650	1.68
6.5x55 MAUSER	140	1,595	1.72
.243 WIN.	100	1,350	1.25
.257 ROBERTS	117	1,280	1.47

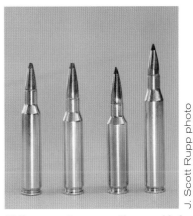

All these rounds are more than capable for taking deer at typical distances—without a lot of recoil (from l.): .257 Roberts, 7mm-08 Rem., 6.5 Creedmoor, .25-06 Rem.

DARE To Be
DIFFERENT

by Brad Fitzpatrick _____

BORED WITH THE OLD TRIED-AND-TRUE HUNTING CARTRIDGES? SPICE IT UP WITH THESE ALTERNATIVES.

I bet I'm not going to shock anyone reading this when I tell you that the .270 Win., .30-06 and the .300 Win. Mag. are all versatile, dependable cartridges that will work on a wide variety of game. Everyone knows that because just about everyone who's ever hunted big game with a rifle has, at some point, been carrying one of these rifles. Every rifle company builds guns chambered

6mm Rem.

This cartridge was introduced as the .244 Rem. in 1955, the same year as Winchester's .243 debuted. Both rifles were conceived as dual-purpose varmint and deer guns, the ultimate all-rounder for the hunter who didn't pursue anything larger than mule deer and who wanted a single rifle to do everything. The .243 Win. won out because it had a slower rifling twist (1:10) that would allow it to stabilize heavier deer bullets better than the .244 Rem., which had a 1:12 twist, and the Remington cartridge gained a reputation for being inaccurate. The .244 Rem. seemed bound for the scrap heap.

Instead, Remington renamed it the 6mm Rem. and gave it a 1:9 twist rate to stabilize those heavy deer hunting bullets. This time the 6mm Rem. caught on, though it didn't exactly catch fire. Fans of the .243 already had their dual-purpose rifle, and they weren't planning to trade it in on Remington's revamped model. The 6mm Rem. did have advantages over the .243—namely a larger case, longer neck for reloaders, and it shot extremely well with heavy bullets. Today it still offers a viable alternative to the .243.

THE RIFLE: Keep your eyes open for used Remington Model 742s in 6mm Rem., one of the greatest rifle/cartridge combos for whitetails and varmints.

6.5x55 Swedish Mauser

If you've never heard of the 6.5x55 Swedish Mauser (or 6.5 Swede for short) you have been missing the boat for the last 118 years. This Scandinavian cartridge was originally designed to be the military cartridge for the Swedish and

for these popular rounds, as well as other stalwarts such as the .243 Win., the 7mm Rem. Mag. and the .308 Win.

Sometimes, however, you just want to step away from the guns of the masses for a moment, to explore new territory in the world of sporting rifles. Maybe you want to walk into the local hardware store and see that there aren't 15 boxes of ammo for your particular rifle. Perhaps you want to draw a crowd at the range, the same

crowd that's used to you dutifully dialing in your trusted '06 every fall as you prepare to head to the deer woods. Maybe it's the rifle shooter's equivalent of a midlife crisis, the ballistic counterpart to the yellow Porsche convertible.

The good news is that there are several rounds as versatile, powerful and accurate as the popular .270, .30-06 and 7mm Rem. Mag. Are they better than these tried-and-true game getters? No, but they're worthy alternatives.

Norwegian military forces. As with other military cartridges such as our .308 and .30-06, the 6.5x55 became a top choice for hunters in Scandinavia. The game of choice was often moose, which certainly tested the limits of the 6.5 bullet. However, the 6.5 Swedish Mauser proved capable of killing the big deer, and the cartridge has certainly accounted for more moose in Finland, Sweden and Norway than any other single cartridge.

Military surplus rifles began landing on American shores, and hunters began taking notice of the 6.5 Swede's mild recoil, accuracy and game-killing prowess. It drives a 120-grain bullet at about 2,800 fps, while the average 140-grain load travels somewhere in the neighborhood of 2,650 fps.

There are probably better varmint cartridges than the Swede, though it works just fine for that application. Where the 6.5x55 really shines is in the deer woods. It produces mild recoil and has a relatively flat trajectory, making it a superb choice for a whitetail hunt. Howa, CZ and Sako are all currently importing rifles chambered in 6.5x55, and ammo is being loaded by Federal, Hornady, Nosler, Norma, Winchester and several other companies.

THE RIFLE: CZ's 550 FS with its Bavarian–style Mannlicher stock chambered in 6.5x55 is beautiful, functional and unconventional. Shoot it once and you'll probably be thinking about that cartridge/rifle combo every time you head to the woods.

.308 Marlin Express

The .308 Marlin Express came on the scene in 2007, a novel idea wherein the .307 Winchester could be used as a platform to create a cartridge that would allow a lever gun cartridge to approach .308 Winchester trajectory and energy levels. The addition of Hornady's Flex Tip bullets meant that pointed rifle ammunition could be loaded into tubular magazines.

Frankly, I don't know why the .308 Marlin Express isn't more popular than it is. Die-hard bolt action fans never made the leap to lever guns, and traditionalists don't seem inclined to try a new cartridge, even if it beats the old .30-30 to death ballistically.

However, the .308 Marlin is a very good lever cartridge, accurate and powerful. It is capable of greatly extending the range of traditional lever guns and has the energy to take just about anything in North America. Recoil is manageable, and Hornady's bullets perform well on deer, black bear, hogs and the like. If you've ever considered a lever gun, this is a very good place to start. Plus, the hard-core bolt action guys at your shooting range aren't going to be happy when a lever-action rifle will shoot sub-m.o.a. groups and their turnbolt rifles won't. Simply smile and shrug.

8mm Rem. Mag.

Do take note of how many cartridges on this list are metrics. For the most part American shooters have dug their heels in on metrics, with the notable exception of the 7mm magnums and the current 6.5mm craze. However, the 8mm Rem. Mag. never caught on after its introduction in 1977.

Why? Well, the first problem is the metric nomenclature. Remington certainly thought fans of the 7mm Rem. Mag. would see the 8mm magnum as a natural step up on power. That wasn't quite how it worked out, though. The cartridge necessitates a full-length, .300 H&H-length action and generates hefty recoil, and consumers weren't running out in droves to pick up the new 8mm magnum.

Despite stiff competition from below (.300 magnums) and above (.338s), the 8mm Rem. Mag. is a performer. It will drive 180-grain bullets over 3,200 fps, and even with heavy 220-grain loads velocities approach 3,000 fps. Full-power 220-grain loads generate in the neighborhood of 4,300 ft.-lbs. of energy, making it a formidable cartridge for heavy game.

For a shooter who can handle the round's hefty recoil, this

DO TAKE NOTE OF HOW MANY CARTRIDGES ON THIS LIST ARE METRICS.

THE RIFLE: Marlin's 336 XLR comes with a laminated stock, stainless barrel and action and a five-shot tubular magazine. When chambered in the .308 Marlin Express this is the archetype go-anywhere, do-anything lever gun.

cartridge is extremely versatile. Lighter loads make it a superb long-range rifle for game such as antelope and sheep, and with well-constructed bullets it will kill deer with very little meat damage. Where the big 8mm shines is on

Okay, we cheated here: The Remington Model 750 isn't chambered in 6mm Rem., but its forerunner, the Model 742, was. If you can find one, you've got a great rig for deer and varmints.

CZ's excellent and distinctive Model 550 with Bavarian-style stock is the perfect platform for the 6.5x55 Swedish Mauser, a gun and cartridge sure to turn heads at the range.

elk, moose and plains game like eland and roan.

Despite its credentials, the 8mm Rem. Mag. is suffering heavily, and the introduction of the .325 WSM didn't help. But those who still stand by the "great 8" claim it is the perfect heavy gun in a two-rifle North American battery and without equal on large plains game in Africa. I can't disagree.

THE RIFLE: 8mm Rem. Mags. are hard to find, but you can pick up a Model 700 Classic or a Custom Shop gun from time to time. I let a 700 Classic with walnut stock and iron sights slip by me at a gun shop a few years back, a move I've regretted ever since.

The .308 Marlin Express shown here in the Model 336 XLR, shoots rings around the old .30-30 Win., but so far it just hasn't caught on with the lever-gun crowd.

While it will never eclipse the .375 H&H for dangerous game, the .370 Sako has a lot going for it: shorter action, less recoil but plenty of punch. Now all you have to do is find one.

.370 Sako/9.3x66 Sako

It would have been just about impossible to lay hands on a .370 Sako a few years ago. However, the company is finally beginning to offer these rifles through its U.S. dealers, and the .370 Sako will likely start popping up more and more as time goes by.

Also known as the 9.3x66 Sako, the .370 Sako is a powerful medium bore capable of taking large and dangerous game. Nothing new there, right? The .375 H&H will do all that as well, and rifles and ammunition are readily available. But what the grand old H&H won't do is fit in a standard-length action, which the Sako cartridge will. In addition, the recoil generated by the .370 Sako is less than that produced by the .375 H&H.

Am I implying that the .370 Sako will ever unseat the .375 H&H? Of course not. I am saying, though, that the .370 Sako is a viable alternative to the Holland. The Sako cartridge has been used on Cape buffalo and other heavy game effectively, and its lighter weight and reduced recoil make it a sensible alternative to the .375 H&H for hunting large plains game species. It is also a great bear, moose and elk cartridge for the United States.

The .370 Sako will drive a 286-grain bullet at 2,550 fps, generating 4,129 ft.-lbs. of muzzle energy. Federal loads .370 Sako ammo with Swift A-Frames, Barnes Triple-Shock X Bullet and Barnes Banded Solids—all with 286-grain bullets—in its Cape Shok ammo line.

THE RIFLE: Sako's Model 85 Deluxe Classic with iron sights. It's not cheap, but it's well-made and gorgeous. That is, if you can find one.

FILLING THE GAPS

by Craig Boddington ———

In recent years I've often written that we have enough cartridges—in some ways, too many. We all know about the huge spate of new "magnums" that have come down the pike in, say, the last 15 years. Some of these have already fallen by the wayside. This doesn't mean they weren't good cartridges. They did exactly what their makers intended them to do, but clearly this wasn't enough for commercial success. Some of the failed ones essentially duplicated the performance of existing popular cartridges or were introduced in caliber fields that were already crowded.

The last couple of years we've seen a slight slowing of new commercial cartridges, although development continues for the AR platform in particular with such rounds as the .300 BLK, .30 Rem. AR and others. To a lesser extent there have been rounds designed to improve the lever gun's capability: the .308 and .338 Marlin Express, and the .475 Turnbull.

While these developments are important, I'd call them "niches" rather than genuine gaps. Winchester's failure with its Super Short Magnum family should provide storm warnings for all manufacturers. It seems to me that, in conceptualizing a new cartridge for factory production by a major manufacturer, at least three criteria should be met.

First, a new factory cartridge needs to meet its intended performance characteristics without pressure concerns and in a package that can be manufactured with relative ease. For instance, there are lots of wildcat cartridge designs in .17, .20 and .22 centerfire that exceed the performance of existing cartridges. But in order to significantly exceed existing velocities, pressures must often be raised above levels that American industry standards are happy with, and in order to demonstrably enhance accuracy, manufacturing tolerances must be tightened to levels that may not be practical.

In other words, some very good cartridges need to remain the province of wildcatters, handloaders and small, almost custom manufacturers who are able to realize their potential. American manufacturers who wish to create a

L.-r.: .250 Savage, .257 Roberts, .25-06 Rem., .25 WSSM, .257 Wby. Mag. The .25 caliber lineup seems full, and only the .25-06 has genuine popularity, but there might be room for a .25-08.

new cartridge generally go through extreme engineering and testing protocols so their cartridge will meet the Sporting Arms and Ammunition Institute guidlines and be accepted as a standard factory cartridge. This costs considerable time and money, and the reality is that many good wildcat cartridges, even with the investment, are too far out on the ragged pressure edge to be accepted by SAAMI.

Second, it must be readily adaptable to existing rifle platforms. Again, not to pick on anybody, but I think this was a major problem with the WSSMs. The cases were too short and stubby to feed properly in many existing actions, and few if any repeating actions were sized perfectly.

Had they caught on, then stubbier, wider actions would probably have been developed, but this didn't happen, so it seems that compatibility with existing rifle actions (as many as possible) is probably a good idea.

Third, for commercial success, a new cartridge should be designed to fit an existing, ready and eager market. In other words, no matter how good an idea it seems to be, folks still have to buy it in order for it to succeed. Considering the huge array of factory cartridges currently available, it appears there are very few gaps remaining to be filled. But maybe, just maybe, there are a few.

.17 to 6mm

We can dispense with this lower spectrum of the cartridge rainbow fairly quickly: I don't think there are any gaps wide enough to allow room for commercial successes. The .17 arena is now very crowded, but the .20 caliber field is wide open, occupied only by the .204 Ruger, which has been a stunning success. There are several wildcats and a few proprietaries that may be better in terms of velocity, accuracy or both, but are they enough better to justify their existence, and can they maintain this edge when commercially manufactured to SAAMI specifications? I doubt it.

Ditto for the .22 centerfires. There are better wildcats out there, but the .223 Rem. and .22-250 Rem. are so entrenched and so popular that even the .222 Rem. and .220 Swift—both awesome cartridges—are barely hanging on. The .223 WSSM died an early death, the .221 Rem. Fireball is a rare bird and so forth.

Pretty much the same should be said for the .243/6mm group. There aren't many cartridges, but only the .243 Win. retains serious popularity. The .240 Wby. Mag. is a rare bird that never made it beyond a Weatherby proprietary. The 6mm Rem. is probably a better cartridge than the .243 Win., but it barely hangs on. The only recent attempt at a 6mm cartridge, the .243 WSSM, was faster and probably inherently more accurate, but it died. If I were a manufacturer looking for opportunities I'd look elsewhere.

.25 to .270

Here there may be some running room. The .25 caliber is sort of a niche market; not everybody loves the quarter bore,

The 6.5-06 seems to be popular with many custom riflesmiths. This Reg LeQuieu rifle is just one of several 6.5-06 guns the author has played with in the last few years.

but its fans are loyal. The wildcat .25 WSM (the Winchester Short Magnum case necked down) seemed to have some traction, but it is overbore capacity and limited in appropriate powders. So the .25 WSSM on the shortened case was introduced—and quickly died.

This is obviously a caution for another .25 caliber cartridge, but I think a .25 on the .308 case (.25-08) might have some legs. We love our short actions, and of course the .308 case feeds almost regardless of neck diameter. Such a cartridge would exceed performance of both the .250 Savage and, in factory loads, the .257 Roberts, which is saying quite a bit. The biggest drawback is that such a cartridge would fall right between the .243 Win. (which is wildly popular) and the .260 Rem. (which isn't doing very well), so success is not assured.

The curse of the 6.5mm seems to have abated somewhat. The .260 Rem. is not a hot seller, but the .264 Win. Mag. has seen a slight resurgence. Perhaps more significantly, in specialty markets the 6.5-.284 and Hornady's 6.5mm Creedmoor have done well. So, especially with the great powders we have available today, there may be room for a fast 6.5mm.

How about the 6.5-06? This ancient (hell, it's older than me!) wildcat has been considered by several manufacturers, and I think it's been passed over because of the 6.5mm stigma. But perhaps it's time. The 6.5-06 is not overbore capacity like the .264 Win. Mag., and it is capable of similar velocities (almost but not quite) and performs fine in a 24-inch barrel.

The 6.5-06 remains a fairly common wildcat that lies exactly between the .25-06 and .270 Win. I doubt it would unseat either in a popularity race, but it could become the most popular 6.5mm ever.

How about a short, non-magnum .270? The .270-.308 has been wildcatted forever. It would be slightly slower than the .270 Win. (about the same gap as between the .308 Win. and .30-06) but would be plenty fast enough for most hunting purposes, would fit in a short action with smooth feeding and would beat the pants off the 6.8

Rem. SPC with traditional .277-inch hunting bullets.

The .270 is a wildly popular bullet diameter, but there are only four cartridges: 6.8 SPC, .270 Win., .270 WSM, and .270 Wby. Mag. There is probably room for one more. If not a .270-.308, what about a .270 Ruger Compact Mag.?

7mm and .30

You've got to be kidding, right? There are so many commercial cartridges in both .284 and .308 bullet diameters that it really doesn't matter how much better a new cartridge might be. All that would happen is to confuse things further, with little chance for commercial success. Some of our current 7mm and .30 caliber cartridges will probably die away, and we sure don't need any new ones.

Well, to be fair, there is one perennial candidate: the .280 Ackley Improved. Nosler had done a great job of marketing this cartridge in the Custom line, and it's a dandy, coming very close to 7mm Rem. Mag. performance in a smaller-diameter, unbelted case. The only caution is that this may not be a cartridge suitable for large-scale manufacturing, and I guess you could say the same about one of the several versions of the .30-06 Ackley Improved.

Medium Bores

Well, the 8mm field sure isn't crowded—basically just the 8mm Rem. Mag. and .325 WSM, but since I seem to be almost alone as an 8mm fan, I think we'll move on.

L.-r.: .270 Win., .270 WSM, .270 Wby. Mag. The .277-inch diameter is popular, but these are the only three general-purpose .270 cartridges. Might there be room for a .270-08 or .270 RCM?

Cartridge sales above .30 caliber drop precipitously, but the .338 is probably the most popular over-.30 bullet diameter, with several good choices from .338 Federal to .338 Lapua Mag.

Missing in the lineup is the .338-06, a perennially popular wildcat that was actually submitted to SAAMI some years ago by A-Square. It is thus already a card-carrying factory cartridge, but none of the majors load it—although Nosler offers it in its handloaded Custom line. Performance comes reasonably close to the .338 Win. Mag., and of course it does much better with heavier bullets than the .338 Federal.

I believe the .338-06 to be today's most popular wildcat, with lineage clear back to Elmer Keith's .333

GAP POSSIBILITIES			
Cartridge	Bullet Weight (gr.)	Muzzle Velocity (fps)	Muzzle Energy (ft.-lbs.)
.25-08	120	2,800	2,089
6.5-06	130	3,067	2,716
.270-08	130	2,914	2,452
.270 RCM	139	3,200	3,150
.280 AI	150	3,053	3,105
.338-06	200	2,648	3,114
.400 H&H	400	2,375	5,009

EDITOR'S NOTE: The bullet-weight choices were the editor's, not Boddington's, so don't blame him. Velocities were culled from various internet sources and manuals—plus, in the case of the .270 RCM, a rough estimate from Dave Emary at Hornady. In the case of multiple velocities for a given bullet weight, averages were used.

The .30 caliber field is so full—and so capable with cartridges such as the .300 Wby. Mag.—that the author doesn't think there's really any point to adding a new one.

OKH. I think it would sell as a factory cartridge, and in fact, of all suggestions in this chapter, the 6.5-06 is the one I have the most confidence in, quickly followed by the .338-06.

I'm also among relatively few .35 caliber fans. We actually have a pretty good selection of .35 caliber cartridges, but the only one that's really popular is the .35 Whelen, which is based on the .30-06 case. Missing is a fast .35, but two options already exist: .358 Norma Mag., which is based on the .375 H&H case, blown out and shortened to 2.5 inches; and the .358 Shooting Times Alaskan, which uses the full-length H&H case.

Both are flat-shooting and powerful cartridges, and they're both hard kickers, too. Norma has made multiple efforts to revive the excellent .358 Norma Mag., which is already a factory cartridge. The .358 STA has remained a pure wildcat. A fast .35 would be a fine tool for big bears and Africa's largest plains game, but although powerful enough, it would not be street legal for dangerous game in the many African jurisdictions that set either 9.3mm or .375 as the minimum. So maybe these need to stay where they are.

The 9.3mm isn't yet popular enough in the United States to warrant experimentation, but how about another .375? Well, with options ranging from the mild .376 Steyr on up to the brutal .378 Wby. Mag., I think we have enough choices in this caliber. Years ago, the late Finn Aagaard experimented with a short .375 based on the .458 Win. Mag. case necked down. He got performance close to the H&H but in a .30-06-length action. This was and is a great cartridge—except that the unbelted .375 Ruger is better, and the .375 is such a small market.

.40 and Up

In terms of actual utility, the big-bore market is the most limited of all. But we rifle shooters love our big boomers, and this field is probably the richest of all in wildcats, proprietaries and old-timers resurrected by smaller manufacturers. The problem is that, with dozens of choices, the market for any single big-bore cartridge is extremely limited.

Also, performance levels tend to be boringly similar. For instance, despite all arguments that can be made, there is no appreciable difference in performance

on game between the .404 Jeffery, .416 Rem. Mag., .416 Ruger and .416 Rigby. Take your pick and be happy.

The .458 Win. Mag. and .458 Lott are probably the two most popular true big-bore cartridges (.450-plus), so this is a small field. But if you don't like either, then you can choose proprietaries such as the .450 Dakota or .450 Rigby Rimless, you can step up to the .500 Jeffery or .505 Gibbs, one of the big Nitro Express rounds or a dozen other obscure big bores. There are probably gaps, but is there a genuine need?

As silly as it sounds, what we don't have is a genuine .40 caliber bolt-action cartridge. In double rifles and single-shots the .450/.400-3-inch is the cat's meow. A generation ago Elmer Keith (actually, his team of O'Neil/Keith/Hopkins) developed the .400 OKH, the .375 H&H case necked up to take a .40 caliber (nominally .410-inch) bullet.

More recently Holland & Holland has done exactly the same thing with its proprietary .400 H&H. A 400-grain bullet at about 2,400 fps would yield 5,000 ft.-lbs. This is exactly the same performance as the .416 Rigby/Rem./Ruger, so maybe it doesn't make much sense, but a true .40 caliber sounds kinda cool.

But maybe I'm reaching. Truth is, genuine gaps are awfully hard to find, but I'm sure we'll continue to see brave new cartridges—whether we really need them or not.

L.-r.: .338 RCM., .338 Win. Mag., .340 Wby. Mag., .338 Rem. Ultra Mag., .338 Lapua Mag. The .338 is probably the most popular bullet diameter above .30, and Boddington thinks a .338-06 could be successful.

PART III
RIFLE
KNOW-HOW

THE WEIGHT

by Craig Boddington

WANT TO TAKE A LOAD OFF YOUR SHOULDER? HERE'S HOW TO FIND THE RIFLE WEIGHT THAT'S RIGHT FOR YOU.

On the one hand, rifles are getting lighter and lighter. There's a bunch of factory rifles in the six-pound class, and a couple, like Kimber's Mountain Ascent and short-action Adirondack, tip the scales at five pounds or less. On the other hand, rifles are also getting heavier, with "tactical" and "long-range" versions at twice that weight and more. For instance, have you ever seen a light .338 Lapua? Would you want to? It's an old discussion, but with a new wave of both ultra-lightweights and ultra-heavyweights, the question remains worth asking: Is there an ideal rifle weight?

Only you can answer how much weight you want to carry. It depends on your age, physical condition and physical size. Regardless of strength, a heavy, long-barreled rifle is more unwieldy for a five-footer than for a six-footer. But it also depends on what you're doing.

Kenny Jarrett's concept of the "beanfield rifle" made him famous. It was a long-barreled, fairly heavy rifle intended primarily for the stand hunting millions of whitetail hunters do, with the intent to provide accuracy and reach across, well, soybean fields. But was that a rifle a serious mountain hunter wanted to carry to the roof of the world? Some did, but some customers loved Kenny's accuracy but hated the weight, and in time his rifles got lighter.

Of course, there's hunting and then there's hunting. You can probably get a heavy rifle to almost any deer stand. You can carry one in a vehicle, and you can carry one in a saddle scabbard—provided you don't plan on getting too far from your horse. It's a different story on a backpack sheep hunt or almost any spot-and-stalk Western hunt. You definitely want a rifle with enough capability to get the job done, whatever that job is, but you don't want to pack so much rifle that you wear yourself out.

The first thing to realize is that heavy rifles are not inherently more accurate than light rifles, although they are more stable. We'll talk more about barrels in a bit, but it is almost impossible to have a light rifle with a heavy barrel, and a heavy rifle will almost certainly have a fair amount of weight in the barrel. Heavy barrels are not more accurate than pencil-thin tubes. They are, however, generally less finicky because they don't vibrate as much. They are not as subject to the vagaries of bedding, often more tolerant of the range of loads they will shoot well, and of course, they heat up more slowly and therefore will generally sustain a

longer shot string without the bullets starting to "walk."

While these things may be critical to a sniper or varmint hunter, none of them makes much difference to a big game hunter. A good barrel is a good barrel, regardless of weight. A thin barrel is unlikely to hold a five-shot group, but it will certainly hold a two- or three-shot group, and that's generally all you need. So, from a hunter's standpoint, there is no real reason to carry a heavy rifle just for the sake of accuracy.

Stability, however, also applies to the shooter. It is a longstanding article of faith that it's easier to shoot a heavier rifle, especially when you're tired, out of breath and under pressure. I have always accepted this as

gospel, but in discussing this story, editor Scott Rupp told me he wasn't so sure about that. This gave me pause because while Scott never toots his own horn, he is one of the finest rifle shots in the industry, and as a former member of the Army shooting team, he has the credentials.

Maybe if you're a good shooter rifle weight doesn't play a big role. Experience and practice count, but exactly how you shoot also makes a difference. If you consistently shoot from a steady rest—whether over a daypack, off a bipod or from the rail of a treestand—it probably doesn't matter. For me, however, when an unsupported shot is all that's available, I find a heavier rifle settles in

Heavy rifles aren't more accurate than light ones, but they tend to be easier to shoot well in the field. Shooting from a solid rest can narrow that gap, though.

Boddington took this blue sheep at 16,000 feet elevation with a Blaser in .300 Wby. Mag. that weighs 9.5 pounds with everything on it and in it. While such a weight may be more than some are willing to carry, he likes the capability he gets from the rig.

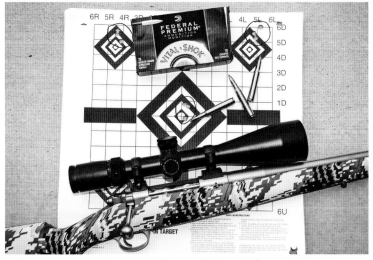

A Kimber Mountain Ascent in .30-06 is super-light and will carry nicely, although its light barrel will heat up quickly—a consideration at the range but likely not in the field.

better and quicker and wobbles less than an ultra-lightweight.

Light rifles certainly kick more. Felt recoil depends somewhat on stock fit and design, and it's certainly mitigated by a good recoil pad. However, recoil is a classic example of Newton's Third Law of Motion regarding "equal and opposite reaction," and without weight to slow this reaction, a lighter rifle produces more recoil than a heavier rifle firing the same cartridge. A six-pound .30-06 kicks a whole lot more than an eight-pound .30-06, and I don't care who you are: a six-pound .300 magnum isn't fun.

The simplest way to mitigate recoil is to add gun weight. As mentioned, gun weight may also add

Jack O'Connor thought a 7.5-pound total weight was just about right, but he shot a small scope and a .270 Win.—and in the case of the latter didn't have to worry about recoil.

stability, but, again, you have to carry the weight. The second easiest way is to step down in power, which I discussed last issue.

It really doesn't matter how portable a rifle is if you're afraid to shoot it. So if you must have it light and demand the power, then a muzzle brake is a sound option. I don't care for them simply because of the noise, but they work. Hunting partners and guides hate them, but they can attenuate recoil by as much as 40 percent.

A partial solution is the removable brake so common today. Use the brake to practice on the range, where everybody is wearing hearing protection, and replace it with a thread protector when you go afield. Just remember to check zero again after removing the brake. It's a matter of barrel harmonics; some rifles shift zero a bit with the brake removed, others do not. But don't leave it to chance.

Gun weight comprises primarily three elements: action, stock and barrel. Generally speaking, the action is a large chunk of metal, and there isn't much to be done to reduce its weight. Blind magazines—which I really don't like because they collect gunk and are harder to clear in case of a misfeed—are lighter than floorplate designs. Alloy floorplates are lighter than steel.

Short actions are lighter than standard (.30-06) or magnum-length actions. And, of course, titanium is lighter than steel. But if weight reduction is a major issue, then you probably want to start with a short action and blind magazine. The Winchester Short Magnums, Remington Short Action Ultra Mags and Ruger Compact Magnums are all about this. They offer performance close to traditional belted magnums but can be housed in shorter, lighter actions. (Of course, they're gonna kick!)

Stock material and design are probably more important than the action in determining final weight. Synthetics are not necessarily lighter than wood. A trim wooden stock can be very light. A synthetic stock of solid construction will be heavier than a synthetic stock that's foam-filled and can be heavier than wood. Laminated stocks, though probably the strongest, are generally the heaviest.

Just for fun I weighed several stocks. A beefy walnut stock off a CZ .375 weighed three pounds, almost exactly the same as a beefy laminate stock off an E. R. Shaw .35 Whelen Ackley Improved. The latter rifle with blind magazine and light scope weighs nine pounds. With scope the CZ .375 is over 10. At those levels of recoil, I don't want either rifle much lighter.

To illustrate the difference, I also weighed the trim synthetic stock on a Ruger American .30-06. It's about 1.3 pounds, which is quite a difference from the other two. With such an ultralight stock and a light polymer magazine, the Ruger American has a head start on being extremely light. However, it actually weighs a bit over six pounds with bases but no scope due to its fairly massive action and beefy barrel. The barrel is not a bad place to put gun weight. As discussed, a heavier barrel isn't more accurate, but on the range, it sure is a lot easier to see how a heavier barrel shoots. Also, I submit respectfully that six pounds is a pretty good starting point for a .30-06.

However, the barrel is a major chunk of steel, and there are several ways to shave barrel weight. Most obvious is simply a thinner barrel, with drawbacks as discussed. Fluting is more costly and is rarely seen on production rifles, but it's a sound proposition. Fluting removes weight and also expands surface area for more rapid cooling. The raised portions between the flutes also act like reinforcing "ribs," so there is little reduction in the actual stiffness of a fluted barrel. Other than cost, there is really no drawback.

Carbon-fiber-wrapped barrels are another option. A conventional steel barrel is turned pencil thin, then reinforced and encased in carbon fiber. The process was pioneered by Christensen Arms, and my most recent experience has been with barrels from Proof Research. The effect is a stiff barrel much lighter than steel and one that simply doesn't heat up. It's bulkier than steel but light with incredible shot-to-shot consistency. The only drawback is cost.

Another important point regarding gun weight is we spend a lot of time comparing factory specifications, but when climbing a mountain the only thing that really matters is the total weight. A normal sling with swivels and four rounds of .30-06-class ammunition increase gun weight by almost a half-pound.

There isn't much to be done about that, but the scope and mounts add a minimum of a pound, and with bigger scopes all the rage, many optics will add more than two pounds. Scopes with 30mm tubes weigh considerably more than scopes with one-inch tubes. Yes, they gather more light and have a greater range of adjustment. As with everything else, there are trade-offs. If weight is a primary concern, consider going with a smaller, lighter scope, but don't whine if you don't have the capability you want when it comes time to shoot.

Although it's a matter of a few ounces, scope mounts also vary considerably in weight. But no matter what your rifle weighs when you take it out of the box, it's going to weigh between 1.5 and 2.5 pounds more when you scope it, load the magazine, sling it and head up the hill.

So is there a perfect weight? Like so many riflemen of my generation, I often defer to Jack O'Connor's wisdom. He never knew synthetic stocks, but he loved his Winchester Model 70 Featherweight .270s (he had a pair) stocked in trim and fairly light walnut. He figured a "go up the mountain weight" of 7.5 pounds to be a good compromise between portability, stability and shootability.

That's a nice number, but remember: Jack O'Connor almost never hunted big game with a scope larger than 4X with a one-inch tube. No matter how light your rifle starts out, it is difficult to keep it to O'Connor's recommended weight if you prefer a 30mm scope with high magnification and large objective. Also, O'Connor was a .270 guy, thereby limiting how much recoil he put up with. He certainly wasn't wrong. There isn't much you can't do with either a .270 Win. or a fixed 4X scope.

But some of us have more confidence in greater power and/or flatter trajectory, and today the majority of us want more scope. If you started with a five-pound rifle and put a substantial scope on it, you'd wind up within O'Connor's recommended window.

Sometimes I want more capability, and it comes at a price. One of my long-time favorite rifles is a .300 Wby. Mag. on a left-hand Winchester Model 70, built by Lex Webernick. Although fluted, it has a stiff 26-inch barrel without muzzle brake. Weight with mounts but without scope is right at eight pounds. With a variable scope and a one-inch tube, we're up to nine pounds. Load it and sling it and we're up to 9.5 pounds. It has gone up an awful lot of mountains exactly that way, and while I wish it was lighter, at that weight recoil is very manageable, and it's easy to shoot well.

I've carried considerably heavier rifles up a lot of mountains, but I don't want to do that anymore. These days, I'm actually trying to cut down, but I like our modern optics, and despite Scott Rupp's pessimism, I still prefer the stability of a slightly heavier rifle.

In recent years I've done a lot of mountain hunting with a Blaser R8, also in a .300 Wby. Mag. barrel with a full-size scope. I realized in working on this chapter I'd never weighed it, and when I did, I found it's right at 9.5 pounds in full hunting mode. Apparently, this is a weight I'm willing to carry to get the capabilities I don't necessarily need but that give me confidence.

I do not suggest you should do as I do. Conceptually, I think O'Connor had it right at 7.5 pounds, and at my age, I'm out of my mind to haul a 9.5-pound rifle up anything steeper than my driveway. But with the optics we prefer today, I think it's difficult to get out the door at O'Connor's recommended weight. If you prefer a more powerful cartridge, you probably need a bit more weight anyway, but it is totally unnecessary to carry as much gun weight as I often do.

Today, there's probably a happy medium in the eight- to 8.5-pound class all set and ready to go. But, understand, whether we're talking .270 or .300, I'm speaking here of a general-purpose hunting rifle. A dangerous game rifle is an altogether different kettle of fish. It should probably start at about 9.5 pounds with a .375 and work up as caliber increases.

A LIGHT **BRIGADE**

Three custom guns that illustrate the pros and cons of lightweight rifles.

BY CRAIG BODDINGTON

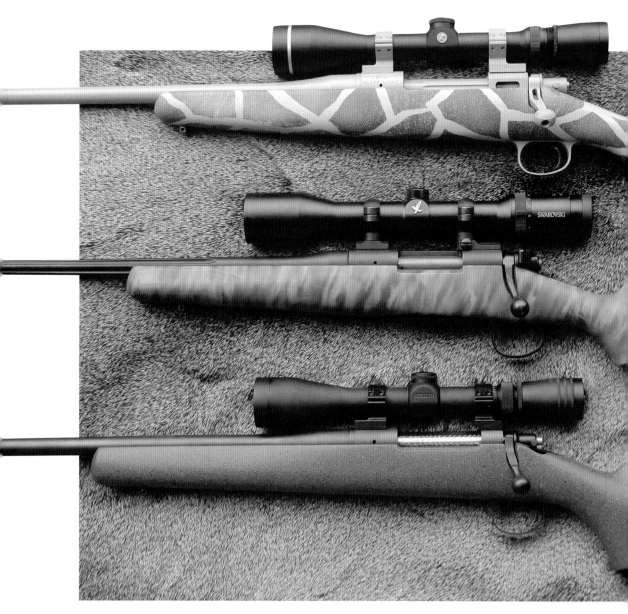

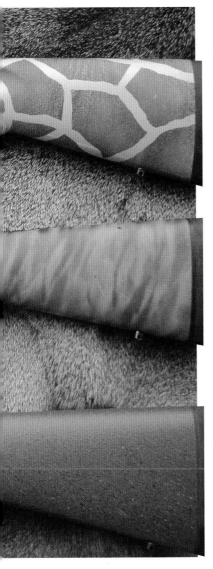

My favorite hunting rifles have always been fairly heavy, with a lot of the weight in long, stiff barrels. The weight dampens recoil and makes them easy to shoot on the bench—and also makes them come steady quickly from field positions. The heavier barrels also heat up much more slowly, which helps when testing loads at the bench.

It is often believed that heavier barrels are more accurate than light barrels. I am certain this is not true. The quality of a barrel is the single most important factor in rifle accuracy. How much steel surrounds that perfectly cut chamber and rifling is not, in itself, of critical importance. However, it is definitely more difficult to get a light barrel to shoot its best.

In my experience, light barrels are more finicky about bedding and thus are likely to be more finicky about the loads they shoot best. Barrel heat is also a significant factor. Slim barrels heat up quickly, the metal expands, and the groups start to wander.

A pencil-thin barrel may not be capable of firing a five-shot group without stringing (usually vertically). If you really want to know the true accuracy potential of a light barrel, the best way is to fire a shot, then wait for the barrel to cool completely, fire again, and etc.

This takes a great deal of time and, on a hunting rifle, probably isn't particularly meaningful. After all, if your first shot isn't exactly where you want it to be, you don't have time for the barrel to cool before you shoot again. Being lazy and chronically short on time, I go with three-shot groups.

Like I said, heavier barrels tend to be easier to shoot from the bench and in the field, but you do have to carry that weight. For many years I had no concern about gun weight, even on serious mountain hunts. Today, in my late 50s, nothing comes quite as easy. There is no way I'm going to haul another 12-pound rifle up another mountain, finally recognizing I can get up the mountains more easily—and shoot better when I get there—with a lighter rifle.

So if you're in the same boat as me or just like light rifles, the question becomes: Just how accurate can they be?

Given the mindset we have that heavy barrels are more accurate, I do think our expectations are more reasonable with light rifles. Since we tend to put smaller scopes on light rifles—and since, being light, they kick harder and thus are more difficult to shoot—this is often a self-fulfilling prophecy.

Does it have to be that way? The single most important components to accuracy is a good barrel, proper assembly (sound bedding, true mating of action to barrel) and good ammunition. Cartridge design and rigidity of action are also factors but aren't as influential as the first three.

Since there are so many variables that go into it, I'm going to take you through three light rifles I happen to have some experience with. All three are "conventional" hunting rifles, with synthetic stocks and "normal" barrel lengths.

One is a Match Grade Arms Ultra-Light .270 Winchester, made by Kerry and Carol O'Day in Spring, Texas. It's the lightest of the three—weighing 6.4 pounds with Leupold Vari-X III 3.5-10X scope in Talley lightweight one-piece base and rings.

I think the total weight of the rifle is the most important figure,

The Ultra Light Arms action is a push-feed action, its primary difference being that it's as trim and light as possible. A slight additional weight-saving is gained by the very light Talley mount, a one-piece base with split ring.

The Match Grade Arms rifle achieves much of its weight reduction by removing metal from—"skeletonizing"—the action. The bolt is fluted, and metal has been removed from the bolt handle as well.

and the Model 700 action on which it's built is skeletonized: The bolt is fluted, and the sides of the action have cutouts to remove metal. There's even a cutout in the bolt handle, with the bolt knob itself hollowed out.

The barrel is slender, but I wouldn't call it pencil-thin. Length is 22 inches, and although it tapers quickly ahead of the action, it still retains a .625-inch diameter at the muzzle. The barrel is free-floated down to the major barrel taper ahead of the action, with the rest of the barrel and the action solidly bedded.

It really likes handloaded 140-grain Nosler AccuBonds. However, it groups identically with Winchester Supreme's 140-grain AccuBond-CT and, interestingly, puts Federal Premium's 130-grain Barnes Triple Shock into the same tight group. With any of these loads we can count on three-shot groups under an inch, and on a good day I've seen these cut in half.

There is one strange thing about this rifle: It is pressure sensitive. For example, we get very hard extraction and flattened primers with Hornady Custom 130-grain loads, but this rifle digests the Hornady's new Superformance load without a hiccup and shoots them very well. Most recently, I borrowed this rifle for a hunt in Turkey and shot a big Anatolian stag at nearly 400 yards. The little .270 put the Superformance GMX bullets right where they should be, dropping the stag in his tracks.

This rifle has seen much more use than the other two and is one

because to be useful even a very light rifle must wear a good scope. However, this "ready to shoot" weight is influenced by choice of scope and, to a lesser degree, the scope mounts. In this case we have a versatile, fully capable variable scope, but it's a light one at 12.6 ounces.

The Talley aircraft aluminum mounts, base and lower ring in one piece with split ring attaching with four screw, is one of

the lightest (and strongest, and simplest) on the market. They weigh in at less than 2½ ounces. This brings stripped gun weight down to about 5½ pounds.

Just about everything about this rifle is light. The stock is foam-filled and reinforced synthetic. This is my wife's rifle, so the stock is short and the fore-end appropriately short as well. This undoubtedly shaves a few ounces. It has a blind magazine,

The Match Grade Arms .270 has remained both accurate and consistent, although it's a bit finicky about the loads it likes. Hornady's Superformance GMX load shoots well.

of the most consistent and trouble-free rifles we own.

The H-S Precision Pro-Series 2000 SA is no longer the Rapid City, South Dakota, company's most current model, but it remains a good example of this firm's work. "SA" stands for short action, which saves a bit of weight on the 22-inch-barrel .270 WSM.

The action is a CNC-manufactured push-feed with an in-line detachable magazine. This is the only rifle of the three that has a detachable magazine and thus a floorplate. It is also the only rifle of the three to have a three-position (Model 70 style) safety on the cocking piece.

Total weight on this rifle is 7.8 pounds, but it wears the heaviest scope, a Swarovski 30mm 2.5-10X. The scope alone weighs a full pound, and the Redfield-type mounts are also heavy, weighing about six ounces. I wanted the scope for its light-gathering capability, and I don't mind that it adds a bit of weight to the 6.2-pound rifle. Mounting a very light scope would make the little .270 WSM seem not so little.

The H-S Precision rifle has the heaviest action and a larger bolt body required by the fat WSM cartridge. The synthetic stock is beefy in configuration; on this rifle the primary weight savings is in the barrel. The 22-inch tube tapers quickly to .56 inch and is deeply fluted. The feel is thus a bit butt-heavy and muzzle-light, but the stock fits me extremely

well, making it a pleasant rifle to shoot.

H-S Precision rifles carry a half-minute guarantee, and this rifle has met that guarantee most of the time. Generally speaking, with 140-grain loads from Winchester or Federal I can count on it to produce one-inch groups. Recently it has done quite a bit better with Norma 150-grain Oryx loads, a fine choice for heavier game but neither as fast nor as aerodynamic as the 140-grain loads I prefer.

This barrel is fully free-floated, and although the fluting does create stiffness and aids cooling, there isn't a lot of steel in there, and the .270 WSM cartridge is hot and fast. The barrel heats up very quickly.

I have used this rifle off and on for several years now, and it has performed flawlessly. Very recently, however, it developed a problem. Inexplicably, the rifle started throwing the first shot from a cold barrel three or four inches high, then dropping down into a group as the barrel heated. I could understand a slender, free-floated barrel doing this all along, but for a rifle of known accuracy to suddenly do this is beyond my experience.

After I quit swearing and checked all the screws, I tried what is often indicated when vertical stringing is a problem: The good old business card shim between barrel and fore-end, just aft of the fore-end tip.

Yep, that was the answer. Barrels do change as they wear, and any cartridge as fast as the .270 WSM erodes throats and

The H-S Precision inexplicably began shooting first-shot fliers (left groups), but the addition of several business-card shims tightened things up considerably (right groups).

wears barrels. At this point in this barrel's life it wants upward pressure on the fore-end tip to dampen the vibration. Since the barrel had been free-floated, it took fully five thicknesses of business cards to get enough upward pressure. Voila, the rifle responded instantly and was back to shooting the kinds of groups I was used to—without any weird flyers.

If I wanted to be fancy, I could build up that pad with epoxy, or I could just trim the shims so they won't show, soak them in oil to exclude moisture, and then forget about 'em. Either way, this is a very good thing, because I like this rifle and have much use ahead for a light .270 WSM.

The New Ultra Light Arms Model 24, a .280 Remington, is the first of Mel Forbes's Ultra Light rifles that I have ever used. This Granville, West Virginia, company was one of the innovators and has long been a leader in the development of extra-light sporting rifles.

This rifle weighs 6.6 pounds with scope, a new Redfield Revolution 4-12X weighing 13.1 ounces, mounted with the same Talley setup I used on the Match Grade Arms rifle. Scope and the mounts together weigh just under a pound, making the .280's stripped gun weight less than 5¾ pounds.

This is actually quite remarkable when you consider that the .280 Remington requires a standard (.30-06-length) action, and this rifle has a 24-inch barrel. Actually, the fully bedded barrel isn't all that slender. It tapers a bit more gently, and at the muzzle it's the same .625-inch diameter as the Match Grade Arms .270's 22-inch barrel. This is, in other words, a full-size barrel, so the weight reduction comes from elsewhere.

Like most custom gun makers, Mel Forbes doesn't make his own barrels, but unlike many he does make his own actions—a tidy two-opposing-lug push-feed action that is as light as it can possibly be.

The synthetic stock is full-size with a generous pistol grip, but it is also light. In sum there is actually nothing unusual about the Ultra Light Arms Model 24; it is simply a well-made, full-size, synthetic-stocked sporter with a blind magazine that truly is ultra light.

Like the other two rifles, this one has a good trigger, albeit with a wide shoe that feels very good but did take some getting used to.

While it's a great and versatile cartridge, the .280 has never been one of my favorites, and since I hadn't shot one in awhile I didn't have any ammo on hand and was only able get two loads for my initial testing: Federal 150-grain Nosler Partition and Winchester with 140-grain Ballistic Silvertip.

Initial groups were disappointing at about 1¼ to 1½ inches. This suggests at least three lessons about all rifles, not just light rifles: No rifle should be judged until a wide selection

The author has come to the realization that carrying a light rifle can actually help his field shooting. He took this Anatolian stag with a Match Grade Arms .270 and Hornady Superformance GMX ammo.

of ammo is tried; many barrels need some breaking in; and sometimes a day makes a difference. The following day, after cleaning the barrel, groups with the 140-grain Winchester load were down to 3/4-inch.

A few days later I was sitting on a sandhill in northwestern Oklahoma on the opening day of deer season. At about 8:30 a nice buck appeared 350 yards away and looked like he was going to disappear over a ridge. I had a good rest, but I had expected closer shots and had zeroed the rifle only slightly high at 100 yards. I gave him just a sliver of daylight over the backline, the bullet hit with a resounding "thwack," and he rolled down the sandhill.

This was a very auspicious beginning for a brand new rifle that not only shoots straight but is a joy to carry. And that's the thing about light rifles: They really can shoot straight, although sometimes it takes a bit of work to get them to strut their stuff. They are not as steady or as stable as heavy rifles, but it's a whole lot easier to get them where you need to be to make the shot.

SHOOTING FOR PERFECTION

TIPS FOR SELECTING THE IDEAL RIFLE FOR YOUR NEXT BIG HUNT.

by Craig Boddington

Many hunters view the rifle as a tool, essential but not intrinsically more interesting than a shovel or a hoe. My suspicion is few regular readers of this magazine share that sentiment. To us the rifle is a special instrument, given loving care and fed a special diet that is constantly refined.

When we plan a hunt, while the expedition itself is important, we spend a lot of time trying to figure out the perfect rifle, cartridge, load and sight. Often this is a mental exercise. We envision the exact, perfect rifle for a particular situation, but we choose the closest setup we already have—perhaps mitigating the compromise by working up a new load with a bullet "perfect" for the job at hand. Sometimes we go further than that, using a special hunt as an excuse for procuring a new rifle or scope, possibly to figure out a new load as well.

These are fun exercises serious rifle shooters simply cannot avoid, but there are pitfalls. Remember the adage, "Beware the one-gun man." I would be the last to suggest that one size fits all, but there are clear advantages to using just one or two rifles.

Back in the 1950s Grancel Fitz of Boone & Crockett Club fame became the first person known to have taken all species of North American big game. He did it all with a .30-06, easily the most popular cartridge of his time.

A generation later my friend Dr. J.Y. Jones accomplished the same feat, also with a .30-06. Jones followed up this feat by hunting throughout Europe, Asia and the South Pacific. Again, he stayed with one rifle, but this time he switched to the 7mm Rem. Ultra Mag.

Although total familiarity is an advantage, and I admire the steadfastness, this has not been a school I have followed. I, too, have taken all the huntable North American species, plus a broad selection on all the other continents. It would take me days to figure out all the different rifles and cartridges I have used. So I'm not a one-gun man, but I don't exactly recommend following my lead because my job as a gun writer means the choice of rifle and cartridge isn't always up to me—and the rig often shows up at the last minute, preventing me from gaining familiarity with it.

Timing is key to selecting the perfect rifle. It can't be a last-minute thing. You have to conceptualize the right rig well ahead, then get your hands on it early enough so it becomes an old friend long

before you set it to its perfect task. No rifle—regardless of how much thought you've put into its selection—is ideal if you haven't had time to work out any bugs and become totally familiar with it.

I can't put a time frame on how early you should plan. It really depends on your schedule and your ability to access a range. I suggest a minimum of a half-dozen range sessions—whatever that means to you. (If the rifle is to be taken on a foreign hunt, plan on a couple of range sessions before you reach any gun permit deadlines. Make sure the darn thing works before you commit to using it.) In my experience, final decisions on rifles are best made a good three months before a hunt.

Your planning, though, obviously starts well before this because you have a lot of decisions to make based on what the hunt entails. Size of the animal is important, of course. Most of us would choose a different rifle and cartridge for brown bear than for pronghorn, for example.

However, the nature of the animal is also important. Moose and brown bear are similar in weight, but most experienced hunters would agree bears are tougher than moose. Even if you don't buy that, you can probably accept bears are potentially more dangerous than moose. You could use the same rifle for both species, but an ideal rifle for the biggest bears is probably somewhat more powerful than the perfect moose rifle.

These are obvious, but that's just the beginning. It's equally important to take into consideration likely shooting distances, hunting methods and climate. Nobody shoots big bears at long range. Much moose hunting is done in forested areas where shots are close, but in Alaska, western Canada and our northern Rockies (Shiras moose), the terrain can allow for longer shots.

At the other end of the North American spectrum, a lot of white-tail hunting is still done in thick cover, with little opportunity beyond 100 yards. A .30-30 is just fine, especially if garnished with a low-powered scope. On the other hand, a lot of whitetail hunting is done in agricultural areas, where it's advantageous to be able to reach to 300 yards and beyond. The .30-30 is outclassed, and the ideal whitetail rifle looks altogether different.

How about hunting methods? Gun weight isn't a major factor for stand hunting but is for spot-and-stalk—especially in steep country. In open country, including much mountain hunting, longer barrels are an advantage because they wring out

Bolt actions rule today, but there's still a place for the fast-handling lever gun—whether as a close-cover deer gun or as your faithful companion on a horseback hunt.

a bit more velocity, and there's no penalty for carrying the longer barrel.

In thick cover, however, long barrels can be a pain, and in the confines of some blinds, lengthy barrels can be a real detriment. At five feet nine I'm not a tall guy, but I've always leaned toward longer barrels. Years ago, on a whitetail hunt in Texas from a typical box blind, I carried a bolt action with a 26-inch barrel. It was almost impossible to bring it to bear without the barrel rapping against the roof or supports.

Horseback hunts bring up a whole different set of challenges. Although the bolt action is usually my default setting, the bolt handle is a pain in the saddle scabbard. Semiautos gather a lot of gunk, and a projecting operating handle can also be a problem.

Flat-sided actions such as lever actions and single-shots are most comfortable under the leg, but think it through. A single-shot is either fully empty or fully loaded. When you need to jump off the horse and grab the rifle, there's an extra step with a single-shot in that you have to fumble for a cartridge.

So it's no surprise the lever action can be a good choice for a horseback hunt. And today we have more suitable big game choices thanks to the Marlin Express cartridges (chambered in the Marlin XLR series) in addition to the tried-and-true Browning BLR, which is chambered to several big game rounds.

But, again, for the most part I am a bolt-action fan. One of the things I like about it is the chamber can be loaded and unloaded more quickly and more quietly than other repeating rifle actions. In stand hunting, which many of us do almost exclusively, this doesn't matter. You get into your stand and load the rifle once; you unload it when climbing down. That's different from foot hunting, where you might chamber and unchamber a round a doz-

en times (crossing fences and other obstacles, action imminent and then not) before getting a shot.

And in the case of guided hunts, you're usually hunting with an empty chamber and full magazine, loading only when a shot presents itself. Being able to quietly slide a round into the chamber is key.

Conditions also influence rifle

When it comes to cartridges, we all have our favorites, and we can stand by the campfire and pontificate endlessly about our perfect choices. It's important to pick a cartridge you like and have confidence in, with a trajectory you understand and with power level appropriate for the quarry. Within these parameters there are lots of good choices for any

PERHAPS THE MOST FUNDAMENTAL AND DEFINING CHARACTERISTIC OF ANY RIFLE IS ITS LEVEL OF ACCURACY.

choice. I love good walnut, and I've carried beautiful walnut stocks into some really tough situations. The scratches and dings can be partially repaired and mostly concealed, but they're still there. Synthetic stocks are pretty much impervious to the elements. Laminates won't warp and are probably the strongest of all gunstocks. I love blued steel, too, but stainless steel or tough rust-proof finishes like Cerakote are more sensible in humid climates and coastal regions with high salt content.

given application and generations of experience-based conventional wisdom as to what works.

Let's say, for instance, you decide a fast .30 caliber is ideal for an upcoming hunt. While we could argue the nuances, does it really matter much whether you choose a .300 WSM, RCM or RSAUM? Or a .300 Win. Mag., Wby. Mag. or Rem. Ultra Mag? To the game, not much. The first group of "short magnums" can be made into lighter rifles and will perform better in shorter barrels; the

Barrel length plays a key role. Long barrels will milk the most velocity out of your chosen cartridge, but they can be a real hindrance in box stands or tight cover.

second group will yield more velocity but require somewhat heavier rifles with longer barrels.

All the fast .30s perform wonderfully, but they develop a bit more recoil than many shooters are comfortable with—and develop more power than is really needed for a whole lot of hunting. So, instead, perhaps you prefer a 7mm-08, .308, .270, .280, .30-06 or one of the many fast 7mm cartridges. Or maybe even a .25 or 6.5mm. We could make the same arguments about lighter rifles, shorter barrels, flatter trajectories and more or less recoil, but deer-size animals won't often know the difference.

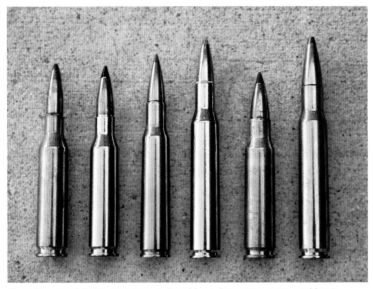

Except for special circumstances such as big or dangerous game, and hunts where really long range is a possibility, standard rounds get the job done: (from l.) .260 Rem., 7mm-08 Rem., 7x57 Mauser, .270 Win., .308 Win., .30-06.

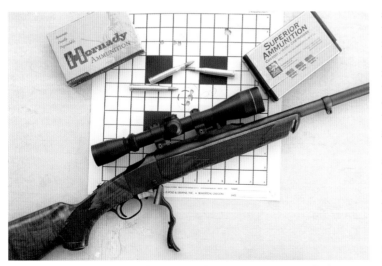

Accuracy is a relative concept. If the hunt is close range, such as deer in the timber or bears over bait, "pie plate accuracy" is plenty. But for typical to long distances you want as much accuracy as you can get.

There are many great cartridges in every power class, with redundant and overlapping levels of performance. It isn't difficult to choose one that has both the power and ranging conditions you need, but you do need to get this fundamental choice right. When in doubt, as in going into an unfamiliar situation, you are probably better off choosing a versatile setup that can handle most everything.

My friend Bob Anderson's several books chronicle the world of sheep hunting. He did a "brother-in-law survey" of 20-some globetrotting mountain hunters. Almost all of them use one or another of the fast .30 calibers.

Again, these are almost never bad choices and, because of their versatility, especially useful in unfamiliar situations, where you aren't really sure what shots might be required. Any .30 caliber is marginal for the biggest bears and not enough gun for Africa's big stuff. There are many choices for both situations, but for the former a scoped .338 makes a good starting point, for the latter a scoped .375.

The perfect rifle must also have a good trigger, but this is also situational. For longer-range shooting you want a crisp, clean trigger that's fairly light. For me, "perfect" is about 2.5 pounds, but a heavier trigger is probably better for fast, close shooting, and you definitely want a heavy trigger on a dangerous game rifle.

Perhaps the most fundamental and defining characteristic of any rifle is its level of accuracy. But this discussion is about choosing the perfect rifle for a specific task, whatever it might be.

Bragging-size groups are always nice, but, realistically, all that matters here is enough accuracy to get the job done. The perfect mountain rifle must be very accurate. The perfect close-cover whitetail rifle must be fast-handling, and the perfect black bear-over-bait rifle must be sighted for low-light conditions, but "pie plate accuracy" is plenty good enough for either of these.

Sights, too, must be perfect for the job at hand. There are still situations where iron sights are superior, but in making such a choice you are often eliminating many potential shots and thus reducing selection, if not actual success.

For instance, I love to hunt Cape buffalo with iron-sighted big bores, but I know going in I have to get fairly close, so I'm eliminating a lot of potential shots. One time I used a Winchester '86 in .475 Turnbull with a classic buckhorn rear sight. We ran out of cover at a bit over 100 yards. Fortunately, I had plenty of time to study the shot, and I got the job done, but the front sight seemed to cover the entire buffalo and several acres around him.

There are some situations where iron sights are in fact the best choice: big game with hounds and elephant hunting. In these cases, scopes may actually be detrimental. However, good old-fashioned iron sights don't work for everyone. As we reach an age where iron sights are difficult to resolve, red-dot sights offer a won-derful alternative for close-range situations.

For most purposes, however, the majority of us will choose scopes. To make a rifle perfect, the scope must also be perfect. When I was growing up, the fixed 4X was almost universal. Like iron sights, it still has a place. Today, however, most of us, including me, will usually choose a variable—low range for close-in work, and a higher magnification range for open country.

I can't tell you what the power range should be because I don't know what you're planning, but keep this in mind: The perfect scope must have enough magnification to simplify the longest shot, but also have low enough magnification to allow close shooting when necessary.

So I've discussed the elements that go, or should go, into your decision-making process. I'll finish up with an example of when I did most everything wrong in hopes you can learn from my mistakes.

The worst choice I ever made was on a Sitka blacktail hunt on Kodiak Island two decades ago. I envisioned thick alder patches, and I was a bit concerned about bears. I was right in choosing a rifle with a synthetic stock and Parkerized metal fin-ish because we were hunting from a boat in a saltwater environment. Then I messed up badly in choosing a .35 Whelen with a 1-4X scope.

Maybe I'd have been okay early in the season, when the cover was thicker, but I went in November. The cover was beaten down and the deer were up on wide-open slopes, and there were so many deer it was difficult to get close to a buck I wanted—too many eyes and noses. My .35 Whelen was outclassed by distance, and the low-power scope made it worse.

As for the bears, well, I was just being silly. I was hunting unguided with no bear tag, and the law is clear that you can't kill a bear in defense of deer meat. We hunted in pairs and kept careful watch, quickly dressing, boning and packing a buck to shore before hunting another.

The buddy system saved my hunt. I managed to scratch down my first buck with the .35 Whelen, but after that I used my buddy's .300 Win. Mag. with a much more powerful scope. I noted that most Alaskan hunters I spoke to used .270s and .25-06s with 3-9X scopes, good choices for most deer hunting and far better than my own choice. I got it wrong because I didn't understand the situation.

BARRELS
By Layne Simpson

&BALLISTICS

Barrel length plays a big role in cartridge performance.

A friend of mine prefers stubby rifle barrels. His favorite deer medicine is a gorgeous little Ruger Model 77 International in .308 Winchester with an 18-inch barrel. As he sees it, the barrels of rifles used by top-ranked benchrest competitors are short so it stands to reason that short barrels are more accurate than long barrels.

Such an opinion may sound logical, but it is far from being true. When the goal is to shoot the smallest groups possible, the diameter of a barrel is more important than its length.

A fat barrel heats up more slowly than a skinny barrel, and heat is what can cause a barrel to wiggle around enough to scatter its bullets over the target. There can be exceptions to

about every rule, but when everything else is equal, a heavier barrel will be more accurate for a longer string of shots.

Depending on the classifications in which they are shot, rifles used in registered benchrest competition have to comply with certain maximum weight restrictions. Examples are 10.5 pounds for Light Varmint and 13.5 pounds for Heavy

Varmint classes. The barrel is made as fat as possible for maximum accuracy, but it is shortened to a length that allows the rifle to meet the weight restriction.

I still have a Light Varmint rifle in 6mm PPC from my benchrest shooting days, and its 21-inch barrel measures .940-inch at the muzzle. But barrels on bench guns are not always short.

The one on my Heavy Varmint rifle is the same diameter but 26 inches long because a rifle fired in that class can be three pounds heavier.

So how long should a rifle barrel be? One answer is just long enough to enable all the powder in the cartridge it is chambered for to burn for maximum velocity.

In some cases that can be rather short. A bullet fired from a cartridge of extremely high expansion ratio such as the .22 Long Rifle, reaches its maximum speed in about 16 inches of barrel. Friction, along with a rapid decline in pressure, in a longer barrel can actually result in a slight decrease in velocity. Target rifles in .22 LR often have barrels measuring 24 inches and longer simply because a longer barrel makes a rifle easier to hold steady in various shooting positions, especially offhand. A bit of velocity loss means nothing in that type of competitive shooting.

Increase the amount of powder behind a bullet of a particular diameter and the charge will need a longer barrel in which to complete its burn. Staying with high expansion ratio cartridges, the .44 Remington Magnum reaches its top speed in barrels measuring 18 to 20 inches while the .444 Marlin needs 22 inches and is still gaining velocity in 24 inches of barrel. The .45 Colt reaches its maximum velocity in the 20-inch barrel of the Marlin 1894, but the .45-70 Government gains speed in 22 inches—and 24 inches is none too long for some powders.

The same rule applies to bottleneck cartridges. I have no idea what optimum barrel length is for the .22 Hornet, but it is probably around 22 inches. The .223 Remington is not bad in a 22-inch barrel, but it gains enough velocity in a 24-inch barrel to make the additional length worthwhile.

Move way on up to the .220 Swift, which burns more than three times as much powder as the .22 Hornet, and 26 inches becomes the minimum barrel length for top performance, and it will actually gain more velocity in an even longer barrel. My Remington 40X-KS with a 27.25 inch barrel is the swiftest .220 Swift I have ever owned.

Burn gobs of powder in a small bore, and optimum barrel length really gets long. A friend of mine has built several rifles on Ruger No. 1 actions in .257 STW, a wildcat cartridge that consumes about a teacup full of slow-burning powder behind bullets weighing 85 to 120 grains.

He started with a 26-inch barrel, then tried 28 inches and is now shooting a 30-incher. Depending on the powder used, each increase in barrel length has rewarded him with a velocity increase of 50 to 75 fps. A Ruger

No. 1 with a 30-inch barrel, by the way, has about the same overall length as a Remington Model 700 with a 26-inch barrel.

It is easy to see that as case capacity increases for a particular caliber, barrel length must also increase if we are to enjoy most of the velocity a particular cartridge is capable of producing. But there is a limit to how much speed will be gained. The 110-grain bullet of the .30 Carbine reaches 1,400 fps in the 7.5 inch barrel of a Ruger Super Blackhawk revolver, and it gains another 600 fps in the 18-inch barrel of the M1 Carbine. I have a Thompson/Center Contender rifle in that caliber, and velocity is less than 50 fps higher in its 22-inch barrel than in the M1 Carbine.

Moving on up in powder capacity, the .30-30 Winchester does just fine in a 18-inch barrel, but since 20 inches is about optimum for it, that's the barrel length most commonly worn by today's lever-action rifles in that caliber.

The .308 Winchester is not bad in a 20-inch barrel, but two more inches increases velocity enough to make the ounce or two of additional weight worth carrying up a mountain. A bullet fired from a 24-inch barrel in .300 Winchester Magnum moves out

The 110-grain bullet of the .30 Carbine clocks 1,400 fps from a 7.5 inch revolver barrel and adds 600 fps in the 18-inch barrel of the M1 Carbine, but little is gained beyond that.

quite rapidly, but once you chronograph it in a 26-inch barrel, you probably won't go back.

Rifles in .300 Remington Ultra Mag usually come with 26-inch barrels because it is about the longest most hunters are willing to carry, but if I were to build the ultimate rifle in that caliber it would be a Ruger No. 1 with a 30-inch barrel.

A fairly larger percentage of today's hunters approve of rifles with long barrels, and for this reason quite a few of today's rifles wear them. But it has not always been that way.

A preference for short barrels among the multitudes of yesteryear is what killed the .264 Winchester Magnum. The Model 70 Westerner in which it was

introduced had a 26-inch barrel simply because the technicians who spent a lot of time and money developing the cartridge knew that to be the absolute minimum length for decent velocities.

Longer barrels were even faster, but decision makers in Winchester's marketing department knew they would be unaccept-

While longer barrels can translate into more velocity and flatter trajectories, their physical dimensions can be a hindrance in tight confines such as box blinds.

Sometimes barrel length is more about utility than performance. When Layne decided to have a .50 B&M Alaskan built, he went with a longer tube to reduce fearsome muzzle blast.

For cartridges such as the .300 H&H, longer barrels on the order of 26 inches allow them to be all they can be.

able to the majority of hunters. And they were correct. After being bombarded by requests for a barrel shorter than 26 inches, Winchester brass finally threw up its hands in frustration and began offering the .264 Magnum in the Model 70 Featherweight with a 22-inch barrel.

In addition to getting the barrel length they had asked for, the complainers got no better than .270 Winchester performance, along with a terrible increase in muzzle blast and muzzle flash bright enough to be seen from miles away.

I first discovered the advantages of a long barrel many years ago when buying a Winchester Model 70 in .300 H&H Magnum. I had only recently become the proud owner of my first chronograph, an Oehler Model 11. The Hodgdon reloading manual I had at the time listed 75.0 grains of H4831 as maximum with a 180-grain bullet for a velocity of 3,013 fps in a 24-inch barrel.

In addition to having a 26-inch barrel, my rifle would take a couple grains more powder without a whimper so muzzle velocity averaged 3,112 fps. Darned good performance considering that the same manual also listed maximum velocities for a 180-grain bullet in the .308 Norma Magnum and .300 Winchester Magnum, both in 26-inch barrels, at 3,022 and 3,128 fps, respectively.

More recently, those velocities came to mind when I decided to have Lex Webernick of Rifles, Inc. build a rifle in .300 H&H around a blueprinted Remington 700 action and one of Dan Lilja's 26-inch, stainless steel barrels with three-groove rifling.

A three-shot, 100-yard group fired by Lex prior to shipping the rifle to me measures less than half an inch. The load, 73.0 grains of IMR-7828 behind the Nosler 180-grain AccuBond, clocked

3,133 fps on his chronograph. The fastest load I have tried in that rifle is 70.0 grains of Big Game and the Barnes 130-grain TTSX at an average of 3,458 fps.

Velocity is not the only issue. When having a rifle in .50 B&M Alaskan built on a Marlin 1895 action, I specified a 22-inch barrel. I had previously shot a friend's rifle in the same caliber with an 18-inch barrel and found muzzle blast to be quite severe.

That's not a problem at the range, but it can be in the field where few of us wear double hearing protection. In addition to being a bit easier on the ears, my rifle is about 100 fps faster with Reloder 10X and the Hornady 500-grain bullet.

On more than one occasion a friend of mine has sworn that he would never be caught in the woods with a bolt action rifle with a barrel longer than 24 inches, and he actually prefers 22 inches. While planning a Wyoming whitetail hunt not long back he informed me that he had never had the pleasure of hunting with a 6.5mm cartridge, so I loaned him my Ruger Model 77 Hawkeye in 6.5 Creedmoor.

Long story short, he bagged a 160-class buck with a single shot, and when he returned, I just about had to sit on his chest and pry my Ruger from his hands. When I asked him if there was anything about the rifle he did not like he gave me a puzzled look. He had hunted with it for a week without even noticing its 26-inch barrel.

Even though I prefer longer barrels on most centerfire rifles,

I am quick to admit there are places where a short barrel does have its advantages. Several box blinds I have occupied through the years spring to mind. Some were so cramped it was about impossible to maneuver a long-barreled rifle for a shot without bumping its muzzle into something noisy. One of my favorites for that is a Model Seven FS in 7mm-08 built by Remington's custom shop back in the 1980s. Another is a Remington Model 600 in .350 Magnum. Both have 18.5-inch barrels.

Friends and I used to hunt black bear with hounds in the Smoky Mountains of North Carolina where the only two directions are straight up and straight down in country choked with laurel thickets nearly impossible to bust through. Short and light was the correct answer to the perfect firearm question, and while I most often carried a revolver in .44 Magnum, I sometimes used a Marlin 336 in .35 Remington.

One of the other hunters had a Model 336 Marauder with a 16.35-inch barrel. Another preferred a .44 Magnum autoloader made by Ruger called the Deerstalker. It had an 18-inch barrel, as did a Remington Model 742 in .30-06 favored by another hunter in the group. The rest had Winchester 94s and Marlin 336s, all with 20-inch barrels in .30-30 Winchester.

I must confess to preferring the looks of a 22-inch barrel on some rifles and I suppose it is because that is what I have grown accustomed to seeing for several decades. To my eyes, the Winchester Model 70 Featherweight would look quite odd with a barrel longer than 22 inches, just as it would with anything shorter. Even so, I would not complain if the barrels on the majority of my bolt-action rifles measured 24 inches and longer.

The opinions you have just read apply to me. For everyone else a rifle barrel should be precisely as long (or short) as they prefer it to be.

THE 10-STEP PROGRAM

Critical things you need to do to get your rifle (and you) ready for any hunt.

By Craig Boddington

Originally I was going to write this as a guide to getting a rifle ready for a "big" hunt, but then I got to thinking: Is there any hunt that isn't important? If it isn't important to you, it's very important to the game animal you're pursuing. I think these steps are universal in application. The order may vary, as will time spent on each, depending on whether the rifle and load you have chosen are old friends or new acquaintances.

The degree of precision required for an upcoming hunt may also alter things. In fact, there are situations where some of these steps may be relegated to a mental checklist rather than physical actions. However, Murphy's Law applies, and I'm certain that totally ignoring any of these steps invites Mr. Murphy as a most unwelcome hunting companion. Lord knows he's been by my shoulder many times—usually when I've tried to cut corners.

1 CHECK FUNCTIONING. If a rifle is an old friend that has worked well for many years, it will probably continue to do so, but that shouldn't preclude inspection for stock cracks and continuous checking that feeding, extraction and ejection are still working.

A new rifle can be more vexing. Having shelled out good money, we expect it to work. Most do, but many don't work exactly perfectly. I've seen sticky safeties, stuck bolt releases and weak magazine latches, but the single most common flaws of new rifles are feeding hiccups. These are often insidious, showing up only when a certain level of magazine loading is achieved.

For instance, because of their short, fat design, the short magnums are devils to make feed properly. I have one that feeds great with one cartridge in the magazine and okay with three, but a second cartridge in the magazine always causes a hiccup.

On a new rifle, thoroughly check safety, trigger and the feeding-extraction-ejection cycle—and check feeding with every possible combination of rounds in the magazine.

Most problems can be fixed, but this can take time. So one of the most important things is to select the rifle well ahead of time, get your hands on it, and make sure it works with plenty of time to fix any problems.

2 CHECK SIGHTS. Even if you're shooting a rifle/sight combination that has been working fine for years, it's still a good idea to check all scope mount base and ring screws for tightness. If you're starting from scratch with new mounts, suck it up and read the directions first. The biggest problem with scope mounts is improper assembly. Screws need to be plenty tight, but if you overtighten and break off a screw, you have a problem.

When mounting a scope, try hard to get the crosshairs perfectly vertical. This is not easy, but a canted scope causes accuracy issues that increase with range. If the vertical wire isn't straight up and down, don't live with it: Loosen the mount and try again until you get it right.

We tend to think of iron sights as more rugged than scopes and mounts. My experience has not borne this out. I've seen front sights bend and rear sights drift and, on two occasions, actually fall off the rifle. Just recently I took my old .30-30 to the range to try a new load. This rifle is a freakishly accurate Model 94 Trapper with a Lyman receiver sight, and I've had it set up exactly this way for 25 years. I have no idea how or when it happened, but the rear aperture was noticeably bent.

3 SELECT LOAD. As riflemen, we want to choose a proper rifle for an upcoming hunt. But since it's always the bullet that does the real work, it's perhaps more important to choose the perfect load.

Thanks to the fantastic array of great bullets available, there are probably many equally perfect choices, but for hunting I think it's best to focus on a bullet that gives you the performance you need for the game you will be hunting. This is obviously different for Cape buffalo than it is for Dall sheep and may be different on elk at long range in open alpine than on the same animal at close range in heavy forest.

We tend to be obsessed with accuracy and velocity. If you're looking for an ideal load for Coues deer at extreme range, you definitely want all the accuracy you can get. If you're going after brown bear in the alders, I submit that a tough, deep-penetrating bullet is probably more important than raw accuracy.

Velocity is also overrated, for two reasons. First, in my experience the fastest loads are rarely the most accurate. Second, velocity is a great enemy to bullet performance. Perfectly good hunting bullets that perform marvelously at .30-06 velocities might become unreliable bombs when

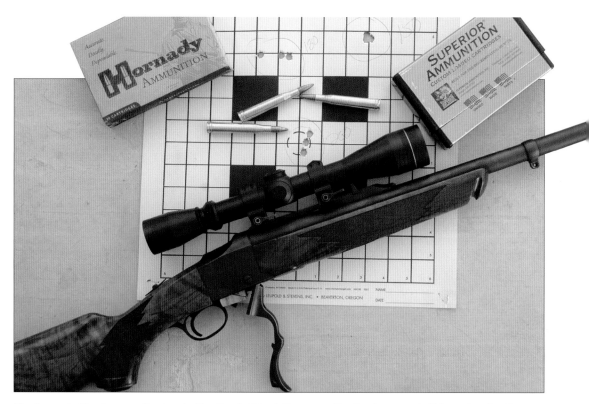

The fun part of hunt preparation is selecting the right load. Pay more attention to proper bullet construction than velocity—and even accuracy in some cases.

pushed at the velocities of the fastest .30 caliber magnums.

On the other hand, velocity flattens trajectory and increases energy—provided you get the accuracy and bullet performance you need and you don't mind putting up with the recoil and muzzle blast that go hand in hand with increased velocity. Most of the time, choosing the right load for a given hunt involves some degree of compromise, and there are usually a lot more good choices than bad.

4 **ZERO AND VERIFY.** Final load selection doesn't have to be done months in advance, but it should be done early enough to allow time for multiple range sessions with that load, especially for any hunt that might require some degree of precision or long-range shooting. Once the load is selected, a decision needs to be made as to how the rifle should be zeroed.

These days it is increasingly common to sight in to be dead-on at longer ranges, as in 300 yards. To each his own, but the most common shooting error on game, and my most common mistake, is shooting too high, not too low. So I generally hold to the older school of zeroing for 200 or perhaps 250 yards, thus reducing the mid-range rise of the bullet.

Of course, I have to start holding over at shorter ranges than if I zeroed at 300 or longer, but that's a matter of knowing the trajectory. Which brings us to the next step: Break out the chronograph and verify the velocity of your load.

Previously I would have said that this is essential only for precision shooting at longer ranges.

With the ballistic coefficient of your bullet and the actual velocity of your load, any good computer program will give you your downrange ballistics. Just recently, however, I saw failure to penetrate on elephant because the loads we were using were fully 200 fps too slow. So now I think it is an essential step to verify the actual velocity of your load.

5 **CHECK SHOOTING AIDS.** Often it's the little things that get you. Trust me, it's no longer a little thing when your front sling swivel stud pulls out and your rifle is catapulted backwards. Mr. Murphy loves this one, usually arranging for the rifle to strike scope-first on sharp rocks. Check your sling, sling swivels and studs.

Also check any shooting aids you intend to use, such as bipods and shooting sticks. It is not unusual for a rifle to have a different point of impact from a fore-end-attached bipod than over sandbags, especially if the barrel is fully bedded rather than

free-floated. Similarly, it isn't unusual for a rifle to shoot slightly differently from a tight sling—obviously because pressure on the fore-end alters the barrel's vibrations.

As your hunt date draws near, you'll want to spend more and more time practicing from your preferred shooting positions, so it's smart to find out early if these cause any fluctuations in accuracy or point of impact.

6 **FUNCTION CHECK AMMO.** I'm not certain exactly when this should be done, but certainly after you've made a final decision on your load and well before departure. One of your final range sessions is probably the right time (and place, for safety's sake)—but not the last one, just in case you need to regroup. Visually inspect every cartridge you intend to take on the hunt, then run it through the action, from the magazine and into and out of the chamber.

With both factory loads and handloads you're looking for

As part of your zeroing, chronograph your ammo. You need to know your actual velocities or any published/computer generated trajectories you have could be wrong.

You need to check your rifle's function—especially magazine feeding, but also safety operation and the like—even if it's a gun you've taken on hunting trips before.

the odd cartridge that is bent or dented (I've even found primers seated upside down.) With handloads, you are also making sure your bullet seating depth and cartridge overall length are suited for your chamber. I have failed to do this step several times. Twice it resulted in a bullet stuck in the rifling and an action full of powder.

Do your function check, and then set aside whatever amount you need for your hunt.

7 **CHECK YOUR GUN CASE.** I'm hard on gun cases, and I've been through several in the past few years. That in itself isn't a problem, but with airline security rules getting tighter and tighter, the airport isn't the place to discover that your case has a

broken hinge or a torn corner. A case deemed defective or unable to be properly secured may not be allowed as checked baggage, and if you're sitting at an airport early in the morning this definitely is a problem.

Soft cases also wear out. I've got several with broken zippers or a hole worn through at the muzzle. This is probably not a panic issue, but once your rifle is really ready for the hunt you want to keep it that way. A good case that properly protects your rifle helps.

8 **PRACTICE FOR THE FIELD.** Practice for the field isn't the same as shooting little tiny groups off the bench. For hunts that require precision and perhaps long-range accuracy, you bet you want to shoot groups.

That should be part of your load selection process. And it's okay to shoot a lot of groups, because tiny little groups build confidence.

Genuine practice for field shooting, however, must be done away from the bench and should replicate the kind of conditions you expect to encounter on the hunt you are preparing for. If you're going sheep hunting, spend time prone, sitting, kneeling, off a bipod, over a pack. If you're going buffalo hunting, spend a lot of time shooting off sticks and a lot more time shooting offhand.

If long-range shooting might be in the offing, this is the time to verify any published or computer-generated trajectories by shooting at the actual ranges you may encounter. Availability of ranges

It's imperative to shoot from field positions—not only because practice makes perfect but also because it will tell you if your rifle's zero shifts when, say, firing from a tight sling.

beyond 200 yards is a problem for many of us, but it's a problem that must somehow be solved if you want to extend your range envelope. One solution is to attend one of the several excellent shooting schools that have cropped up around the country.

9 CLEAN AND FOUL. At the conclusion of the final range session, I clean the rifle thoroughly, and then I fire a couple of fouling shots. It's amazing how far off actual zero some rifles can be after a good cleaning. Some rifles show no difference at all. Me, I don't leave this to chance, and I don't go hunting with a freshly cleaned barrel if I can possibly avoid it.

10 PREPARE FOR THE ELEMENTS. The last details are the little things which, like all little things, can become important. I am not big on scope covers in the field, but they're worth their weight in gold if it's raining or snowing, and they're also good in the vehicle under dusty conditions. Make sure you have covers that fit.

Pack waterproof tape in your gear and put a strip of it over your muzzle in rain or snow. It will not have any effect on accuracy, but rainwater or snow down your barrel certainly will.

If you're going into genuine cold weather, like below 20

degrees, degrease all moving parts and lubricate with just a pinch of dry graphite. On the first day of an Alberta whitetail hunt some years ago I suffered on stand all day, a high of maybe 10 degrees. I was wasting my time; my bolt was frozen solid. I got it thawed and degreased that night—and I've never let that happen again.

Fortunately this was one of the few times when Mr. Murphy was caught napping, otherwise he'd have sent the buck of lifetime right by me.

FOILING FOUL WEATHER

Easy steps you can take to prepare your rifles for whatever Mother Nature dishes out.

By Layne Simpson

The common use of stainless steel in the manufacture of actions and barrels, along with stocks made of synthetic materials, has made it easier for the hunter to head to the hills with a rifle capable of doing a pretty darned good job of shaking off the worst conditions Mother Nature can throw at it.

Even so, such a rifle is not entirely immune to the effects of foul weather. While most stainless steels used in firearms are quite rust-resistant, they contain a small amount of carbon that can cause rusting. I know this from personal experience.

Years ago I took two stainless steel rifles on a rather lengthy hunt in Alaska. As it turned out, I used one for the entire hunt while the other stayed behind with part of its barrel in contact with the wall of an old canvas out-fitter's tent. Since it rained a lot during that hunt, the tent stayed quite wet, and enough moisture managed to wick through its fabric to keep a section of the rifle barrel damp for a couple of weeks. The result was a narrow streak of rust about six inches long. That's an extreme example, but it does prove that some stainless steels are not totally rustproof.

Even though the popularity of stainless steel hunting rifles continues to grow, there are still those of us who enjoy hunting with blued steel and walnut. Back when that's all we had, many of us learned that with a bit of pre-hunt preparation this type of rifle could be made to survive the worst of weather conditions. Doing so took a bit of effort, but it paid off, and some of it came from the manufacturers.

From the practical point of view of a hunter, one of the best things to happen to the walnut stock was the introduction of new synthetic finishes during the 1960s. When introducing the Model 700 in 1962, Remington magazine advertisements made a big deal of the new DuPont-developed RKW finish on its stock. Described in those ads as the "bowling pin finish" (which is what it was originally developed for) it proved to be tougher than nails. Equally important, it totally sealed the wood to prevent entry of moisture.

This is important when you consider that a wooden stock is composed of tiny cells of cellulose that were full of water while the tree was growing. Most of the water is removed from the stock blank during a drying process, and it remains relatively stable as long as its moisture content does not fluctuate greatly.

The finish on the stock of the new Model 700 was not as pretty as the old linseed oil-finished stocks of yesteryear, but when a hunt got down and dirty—and sloppy wet—it was a giant leap forward in terms of practicality.

I bought a BDL grade rifle in 7mm Magnum as soon as it appeared on the shelf of my local gun shop, and even though it has been used hard through the decades its finish is still totally intact. Not once during close to half a century filled with hunts

Regardless of what kind of finish your wood stock wears, a coat or two of stock wax or even good ol' paste wax can bolster protection.

Touch up bare spots in the barrel channel with a polyurethane-based finish to prevent zero-changing moisture from entering the fore-end.

has the rifle lost its zero, which goes to prove that a good walnut stock with proper grain flow and wearing the right finish can be quite stable.

Probably because they are not applied in as great a thickness as the old RKW finish, the synthetic finishes seen on today's rifles are not as durable, but they are still fairly effective at blocking the entry of moisture.

While most companies do a good job of applying the finish on the outside, it is not uncommon to see thin or even bare spots in the inletting. This is easily taken care of by removing the barreled action from the stock and using a finger to apply several thin coats of a polyurethane-based stock finish such as Lin-Speed, Birchwood Casey TruOil or Laurel Mountain Sealer. All are available from Brownells and other accessory suppliers.

Those same products can also be used for sealing off dents and scratches that have broken through the exterior finish of the stock. They may not perfectly match the finishes on all stocks, but they don't look any worse than a dent or a scratch and they will discourage entry of moisture into the wood.

Regardless of whether a stock has a plastic or oil finish, several coats of products such as Birchwood Casey stock wax or good old Johnson paste floor wax will cause water to roll off like raindrops cascading from a duck's back.

A number of products do a great job of protecting metal from rusting, but most I have tried are good for only a day or two of dragging a rifle through wet Alaskan alder thickets. For that, a good wax developed for protecting the finish of an automobile is tough to beat.

Names such as Turtle Wax and Meguiar's Carnauba wax come to mind.

Simply apply a coat, let it dry and then buff the same as you do on your Rolls Royce every Saturday morning. I usually repeat the application a second time or two to make sure I did not miss a spot. The wax job will usually last through a lengthy hunt, and it works on stainless and blued steel.

Extremely cold temperature can cause grease or heavy oil inside the bolt to become dense enough to cushion the blow of the firing pin and cause misfires. Anytime I anticipate Arctic conditions during a hunt, I prepare the rifle before departing home by using bore solvent and brushes to thoroughly degrease the inside of its bolt, along with the firing pin and its spring.

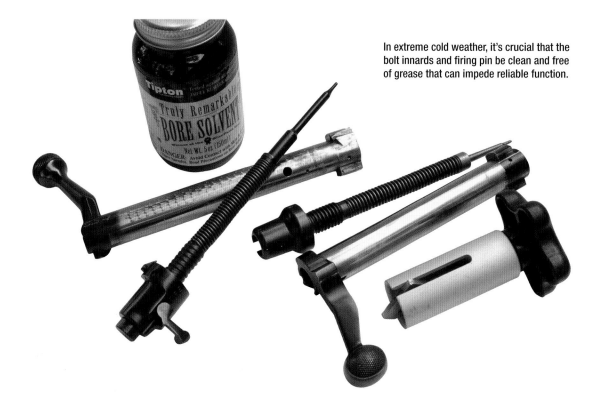

In extreme cold weather, it's crucial that the bolt innards and firing pin be clean and free of grease that can impede reliable function.

This is quite easy to do on the Winchester Model 70; place its safety in the mid position, remove the bolt from the receiver, depress the release button at the front of the bolt shroud and unscrew the entire firing pin assembly from the body of the bolt. The Remington Model 700 bolt can also be disassembled without tools, but a special tool available from Sinclair International will eliminate skinned knuckles (see a review of Sinclair's new Remington 700 bolt kit in this issue's "Lands & Grooves" section).

Degreasing the firing pins of other rifles, especially semiautomatics and lever actions, is probably best left to a good gunsmith, although I find the Marlin 336 bolt to be easy to take apart and just as easy to put back together.

Once I have removed all oil and grease from everything inside the bolt I leave it permanently dry, although at the end of a hunting season I do strip everything down and check for rust if the rifle has gotten wet.

The inner surfaces of the fire control systems of some rifles come from the factory heavily coated with various types of rust preventatives and that too should be removed, especially in and around the various parts of the trigger. A few aggressive squirts of cigarette lighter fluid will flush out the oil, leaving everything dry. The entire trigger mechanism should remain that way, not only to prevent sluggishness or perhaps freeze-up during extremely cold weather but because oil attracts dust,

and that's something no trigger likes.

Placing a swatch of plastic electrical tape over the muzzle of a rifle barrel has long been a standard procedure for preventing the entry of rain, snow, mud, dust and field debris into the bore. Shooting through it has no effect on accuracy because air inside the barrel being pushed along by the bullet will rupture the tape before the bullet makes contact with it. Just remember it goes over the muzzle and not inside where it would become an obstruction.

Also keep in mind that during a heavy rainstorm it is possible for water to creep around the bolt and into the bore where it may collect against the inside of the tape. If water accumulates

A few months prior to writing this, I hunted grizzly in the Arctic, and the rifle carried by one of the Eskimo guides wore a cover. His wife had fabricated it from the sleeve from an old rain coat, and it had Velcro along the bottom to keep it in place. Regardless of how hard it snowed, the scope and action of his rifle stayed clean and dry, even when traveling by snow machine.

Soon after returning home I searched the commercial market for a cover of my own and found it at Middlepoint Trading Co. Called the Gun Boonie, its waterproof fabric has an inner band of elastic along with a drawstring to make it stay put on the rifle and yet it is quick to remove with one hand. It would also serve nicely to protect the scope and action from dust and dirt, like when the rifle is riding in the outside rack of a Land Rover in Africa.

The Gun Boonie covers the scope and action, keeping rain, ice and snow out of these crucial areas.

It offers 100 percent protection when carrying the rifle horizontally with the scope up, but it does not wrap around the bottom of the rifle when it is slung over the shoulder. I will be adding a couple of fasteners at the bottom to make it more like the homemade cover I saw in Alaska. That will make the Gun Boonie quick to remove by not using the fasteners or using them to better enclose the bottom of the rifle.—LS

there and then freezes it will act as an obstruction and possibly cause damage when the rifle is fired.

It usually takes several days for that much water to creep into the bore, but it can happen. On my first hunt for brown bear in Alaska many years ago it rained hard every day, so each night I made it a point to remove the tape and push a patch through the bore with a cleaning rod to dry it out. Replacing the tape readied the rifle for another day of absolutely miserable weather.

If you seal the muzzle of a rifle wearing a muzzle brake and cover its ports as well, keep in mind that bits of the tape can be propelled upward, downward and to either side at considerable velocity. Best place to carry a supply of tape is around the barrel, an inch or two back of the muzzle. Cling-type sandwich wrap will serve the same purpose although it is

not as durable and may have to be held in place by tape or a rubber band.

Other items such as finger cots from your local pharmacy, toy balloons and Muzzle Cots from Birchwood Casey also work quite well. The latter looks exactly like the latex cover the doctor slips on his finger just before he instructs you to bend over.

There was a time when I packed a spare scope on an extended hunt, but today's scopes are so trouble-free and so resistant to internal fogging I seldom go to the trouble anymore. If a spare is taken along it should wear the same type of mounting rings the scope on your rifle has. If the rings are not the quick-detachable type you will also need to take along any tool that might be needed for switching scopes.

Keeping the lenses of a scope free of rain, snow, ice, mud and

field debris is important, and while good covers work fine under some conditions, most I have tried can be totally depended on to stay put when hunting from a horse and the rifle is carried in a saddle scabbard. I prefer a neoprene boot that covers the entire scope and the Scopecoat from Devtron is quite good at that. It is available not only for most riflescopes but for various electronic sights and spotting scopes as well.

If the weather turns from bad to downright lousy, something that covers not only the scope but the entire action of the rifle as well is not a bad idea (see accompanying sidebar). It is not something you would want to have on your rifle when following up a wounded animal, but it is good to have when just getting there and back during bad weather.

GOING To EXTREMES

HOW TEMPERATURE, ALTITUDE AND HUMIDITY CHANGES AFFECT HOW YOUR RIFLE SHOOTS.

by Craig Boddington

A hundred years ago, on an Alberta whitetail hunt, I endured a really nasty cold snap. You'd think the deer movement would be crazy, but with temperatures plummeting far below zero the animals must have been as shell-shocked as I was. I never saw a deer that first day, but when we got back to camp that night I checked my rifle, and the firing mechanism was frozen stiff—no way I could get the hammer to fall. I thawed the bolt out, stripped it down and degreased it (again), thankful I hadn't had a chance at a great buck.

Two hundred years ago I took a Savage 99 in .308 to Africa along with some really good handloads. In those days I was pretty young—bulletproof and invincible like all youngsters. I was inclined to bypass all that silly working up stuff and go straight to the listed "maximum" and did my range work on 60-degree May days.

Over there we caught an unusually hot day, well into the 90s, perhaps more. The rifle's first shot in Africa was at a blesbok, "hit and away," as Ruark wrote. That first shot was also the rifle's last shot in Africa. The fired case was stuck in the chamber and, lacking the camming power of a bolt, the lever was unable to open the action.

For the short term, one of the trackers ran back to the

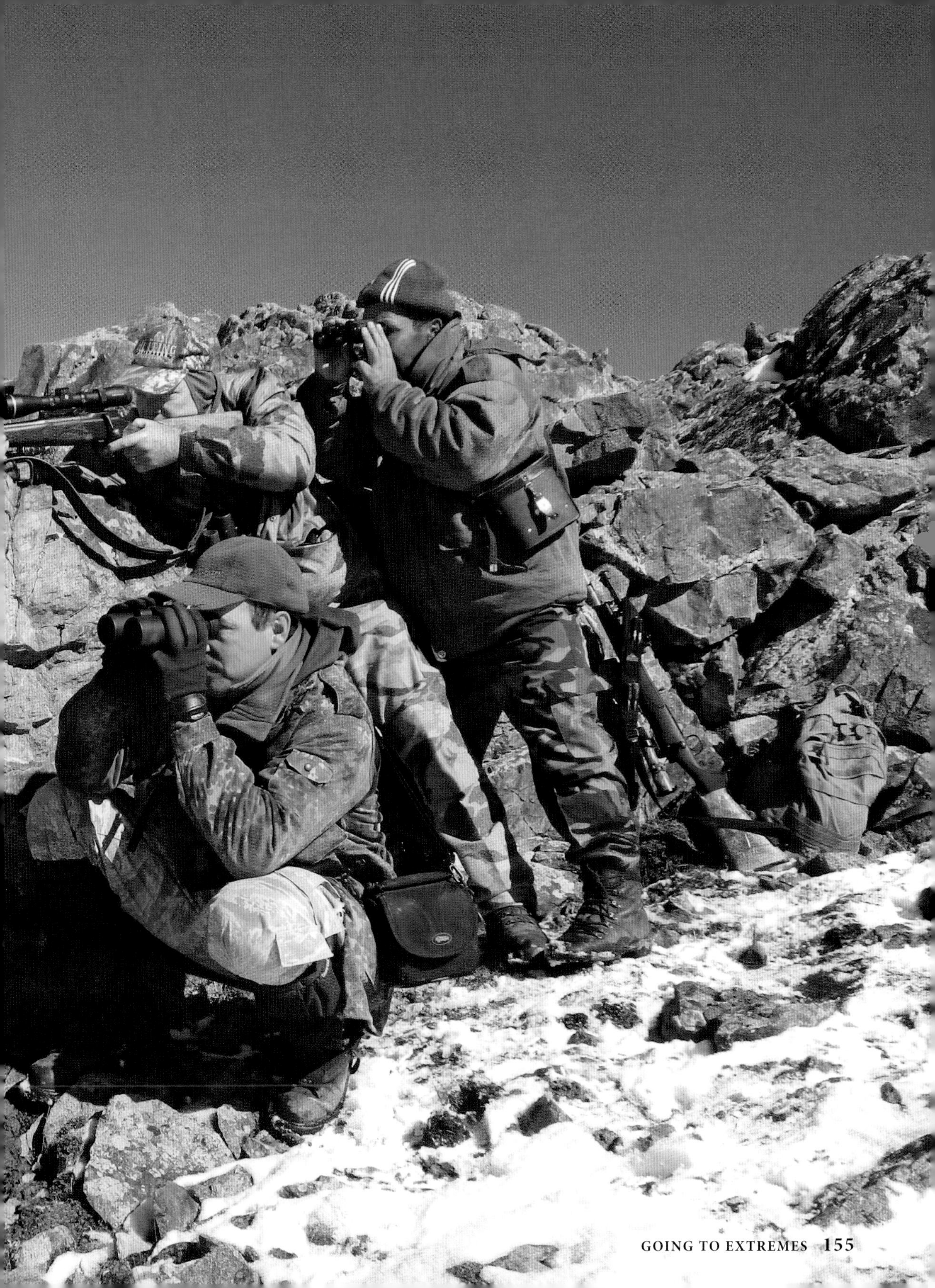

QUICK REFERENCE

TEMPERATURE	
EFFECT	Warmer than home zero, bullet strike up; colder, bullet strike down
M.O.A. CHANGE	0.5 to 1.0 for every 20 degrees of change
ALTITUDE	
EFFECT	Higher than home zero, bullet strike up; lower, bullet strike down
M.O.A. CHANGE	0.5 to 1.0 for every 5,000 feet of change
HUMIDITY	
EFFECT	More humid than home zero, bullet strike up; drier, bullet strike down
M.O.A. CHANGE	0.5 for every 20 percent change

truck to fetch another rifle, and I finished a poorly started job. For the long term, well, that rifle went home with the action closed on a fired cartridge (today there would be no way to get a rifle in such a condition through security) and went back to Savage exactly that way. They fixed it, God knows how.

That's cold and heat. Altitude and humidity are less dangerous in that they are unlikely to cause stoppages, but they do have insidious effect. In fact, any of these factors under extreme conditions will have an effect on your rifle and ammunition, and while you can't always do anything about it, it's important to know what's happening.

COLD I hate cold, and I'm not very good in it. But some hunts have to be conducted in cold weather, and a lot of the hunting we all do—such as North American deer and elk—is generally best when the mercury drops. So deal with it.

If you're headed into serious cold the most important thing to do is degrease all moving parts of your rifle. How crucial this is depends on how cold it is and what lubricants you've used.

Just freezing shouldn't be a problem, and you're probably okay well down in the 20s. Down in the teens, better safe than sorry—but if the mercury plummets toward zero, most lubricants will get sluggish, and you will encounter a slow hammer fall at best—or total lack of function at worst.

Bolt actions are the easiest to degrease and the most likely to continue to function without lubricant. With a bolt gun, remove the bolt and strip it down

Extreme cold temperatures affect you in two ways: One, your rifle may not function as well (or at all); and two, your bullet will drop more.

if you can. If you can't, soak it repeatedly with a degreasing solvent. There are plenty of household or camp products that will do the trick: white gasoline, rubbing alcohol and nail polish remover are good ones.

For other action types, well, it gets tricky. An AR is easy because you can remove all the moving parts and soak them down, but other semiautomatics, pumps, lever actions and single-shots are more difficult. The best course is probably to remove the stock to avoid damage to the finish and soak the action. Some actions can't be guaranteed to work with liquid lubricants, but for the short term you can replace liquids with a bit of dry graphite.

Extreme cold often means snow, so put a strip of tape over the end of your muzzle. I've forgotten to do this a bunch of times, and I usually wind up going under a snowy tree and then spending valuable hunting time digging, blowing and sucking snow out of the muzzle (after unloading the gun, of course). As I and others have written before, a strip of tape over the muzzle has no effect on point of impact.

Depending on the temperature and the distance of your shot, you may need to worry about the effect of temperature on your cartridge's trajectory. The basic rule is: Colder equals more drop. The problem here is that this is a very inexact science because some propellants are more stable across a greater temperature range than others.

There is a rule of thumb. For every 20 degrees difference (and we deal in Fahrenheit here) from the temperature at which you zeroed, you can expect a drop of 0.5 to 1.0 m.o.a. So if you zeroed at 70 degrees and headed to the Arctic for muskox, caribou or polar bear and it was minus 30 when you arrived, you have a difference of 100 degrees. This should mean

If you're hunting in an area significantly higher in elevation than where you zeroed, expect the bullet to strike higher than your original zero.

that your point of impact will be 2.5 to 5.0 m.o.a. lower. This is too great a variance to help you if you need to make a 300-yard shot, so the best plan is always to check your rifle on site, with the climatic conditions you will be hunting under. To hedge your bet, if you are going from warm to cold, you might consider sighting in a bit higher than you normally would.

HEAT Heat has the exact opposite effect, with the same rule of thumb: 0.5 to 1.0 m.o.a. for every 20 degrees warmer than your sight-in temperature. Just remember that rules of thumb are simply guidelines; I've never found any consistency with climatic influences on ballistics. However, it is absolutely true that when ambient temperature increases propellant powder gets "hotter" and produces more velocity, which should raise your point of impact.

There's no substitute for checking your rifle when you get to your hunting location, and if I'm going from temperate or cool to very hot, I usually sight-in dead on and plan to adjust on the ground as needed.

In extreme cold we're worried about the rifle functioning. In extreme heat there's another problem. I said earlier that as temperatures rise propellants get hotter, but what I really mean is pressures increase. I'm sure that's what happened with that Savage 99.

A century ago, when the Brits were loading volatile cordite propellant, they actually offered "tropical loads" that were a bit under-loaded for the English climate but came up to full velocity at the higher temperatures of Africa and India.

If you're going from cooler to warmer, stay away from maximum loads. And don't let your ammunition get overheated. Provided you aren't shooting red-line handloads, ambient

Hunting in extreme heat will raise ammo pressures, so avoid red-line handloads. Higher temps and humidity will also affect your trajectory.

temperature should not be a problem, even if it's over 100 degrees.

Metal such as brass heats in the sun, so keep your ammunition in the shade. Covered ammo pouches are better than open belts.

And it doesn't have to be over 100 outside for temperature to affect ammo. As I write this, it's not even above freezing, and just for fun I put some exposed cartridges on my dashboard, facing the sun. In a half-hour they were almost too hot to touch. It's something to keep in mind.

ALTITUDE This is a chronic problem for me because I live near sea level, but I love mountain hunting. This often entails longer shooting, so small differences in your assumed zero can really mess you up.

Some time back I got one of Leupold's new VX-6 scopes with a custom turret calibrated to a favorite load in .300 Wby. Mag. Of course I had to tell them at what altitude I would be shooting. Historically, I've taken game from 500 feet below sea level in the Danakil Depression to almost 18,000 feet in China. I told them 8,000 feet, which is probably a reasonable average for the altitude at which I'm most likely to use that cartridge.

This is at best a compromise, and just as with temperature, there's a rule of thumb for elevation: For every 5,000 feet of elevation difference between your sight-in elevation and the elevation at which you are hunting, you can expect (you guessed it) 0.5 to 1.0 m.o.a. difference.

At higher altitude the air thins, causing less resistance, so when you go up in elevation the strike of the bullet goes up. When you go down to "heavier" air, your strike goes down. I have not found this rule to be especially consistent, so when you get to altitude check your rifle.

Since I shoot at nearly sea level I usually sight-in at home to be dead-on or just a bit high at 100 yards, and then when I get to altitude I'll be pretty close to the zero I like, which is about 2.5 inches high at 100 yards.

HUMIDITY So far everything we've talked about should be intuitive: Cold, down; heat, up; higher altitude, up; lower altitude, down. Humidity is the exact opposite of what seems obvious. Moist air is less dense than dry air, so if you go from a desert climate to an area with high humidity you can actually expect your point of impact to rise. The rule of thumb: You can expect about a 0.5 m.o.a. change

for every 20 percent change in humidity. And, no, as far as anyone knows, direct precipitation does not impact the flight of a bullet—but snow or rain sure can make it hard to aim.

The bottom line is this: At our home ranges we spend lots of time getting our zeros exactly perfect, and then when we arrive at our hunting sites we generally do a perfunctory check. The reality is we probably won't see a difference of just 0.5 m.o.a, but the size of game animals' vital zones are usually large enough that we can get away with it.

For instance, in Africa there can be extreme climatic changes, but if we're talking a Cape buffalo at 100 yards even the most extreme difference won't matter. On the other hand, a Thomson gazelle out on the short-grass savanna at 400 yards is a much different story.

I've gone over the basic rules of thumb, which will help you know what you can expect, but there is simply no substitute for checking your zero on the ground.

The real rules are: There are no precise rules. So take the time to adjust your zero when you get to your destination. Do it right, take whatever time is required, and get it right.

SCOPE SENSE

RIFLESCOPES HAVE COME A LONG WAY, AND TODAY THERE ARE MORE CHOICES THAN EVER. HERE'S COMMON SENSE ADVICE ON WHAT TO LOOK FOR.

by Craig Boddington

Gun writers are always struggling for story ideas. In our dusty archives you can find stories about scopes versus iron sights, and in the days when scopes were still fragile and cloudy, the aperture sight often won. Even today there remain a few situations—hard rain or snow—where iron sights beat scopes and a handful of dynamic short-range applications where irons and non-magnifying optics (reflex, red dot, and such) trump magnifying riflescopes. In general, however, both science and the people have spoken: Scopes win.

In my own youth, variable-power scopes weren't quite perfected. Reliability was a genuine issue, and virtually all

changed zero as the power ring was adjusted. So, of course, addressing the "fixed versus variable" question was a popular topic. The fixed-power scope usually won, and the pundits would often conclude that a fixed 4X was all the scope anyone really needed. In recent years a couple of my braver colleagues have attempted the same story with the same conclusion, but they are swimming against the tide.

Realistically, many of us need neither high nor variable magnification. We are perfectly well-served by the good old fixed-power 4X, and I'd be the first to say if you don't need more magnification it's foolish to either pay for it or carry it. But, again, science and the people have spoken. The variable-power scope has long been perfected, and the variable is almost universal.

For many years technology limited us to about three times zoom, typified by the long-popular (and extremely versatile) 3-9X variable. This has changed. Four times zoom (as in 2-8X or 4-16X) is hardly new, but today six times zoom is increasingly common—as in 2-12X, 3-18X, 4-24X and so forth—and some brands offer eight times zoom.

Just remember that magnification is just one factor. Quality of lenses and coatings and precision of assembly are of at least equal and perhaps greater value in determining how well you actually see when you look through a riflescope. One must use caution in trying to

oversimplify, but I figure there are three basic classes of variables. Here's a look at them.

Variable Ranges

The low range has low magnification starting at 1X (no magnification) or, in my opinion, no more than 2X. Actually, with today's higher zoom capability, this class is perhaps better defined by its upper end, which I reckon stops at 6X. This class of scope is thus compact and fairly light—depending on tube diameter, construction, and bells and whistles, such as lighted reticles and battery turrets. Most scopes in this group have straight objectives the same diameter as the basic tube, so objective lens diameters limited by tube size (generally one inch or 30mm, although larger 34mm tubes are not new and are being seen more frequently).

In the classic form we thought of this scope as the "dangerous game" scope, but today, we frequently see some of these scopes crossing into the close-quarter combat, tactical arena. This class is indeed ideal for large dangerous game, some bear hunting and a whole lot of situations where the shooting is fast and close.

The advantage of this class is that because the optic lacks a large objective bell and is generally fairly short, the low-range variable can be mounted extremely low on most rifles (including ARs and all rail mounts) and rarely will interfere with barrel-mounted rear sights. Although height of comb obviously matters, low scope mounting allows fast, natural sight acquisition.

The disadvantage is that all things being equal, it is scientifically impossible for a scope with a straight objective to gather as much light as a scope with a larger objective. On a level playing field of like quality (glass, coatings and such) and tube diameter, the "brightness" of this class of scope is limited, and such scopes are poor choices for situations where shooting in low light is likely—such as most whitetail hunting and specialized situations like black bear and leopard over bait.

Greater magnification is often not needed, but just a few extra seconds of visibility can make the difference between a shot and no shot. If this is the case, then the low-range variables are poor choices.

Especially with today's expanded zoom capability, the medium-range variables cannot be precisely defined by lower-end magnification. For instance, this group probably begins with the good old 2-7X but certainly includes the newer 2-12X. On the other hand, with the zoom capabilities we have now, it's hard to put a cap on the high-end magnification.

I'm generally thinking of riflescopes that have low-end magnification low enough that you can't get into trouble at close range. A low-range of 2X or 3X should allow close shooting in the thickest cover, but if you shoot a scope with both eyes open even 4.5X shouldn't cause a close target to be lost in a blur of texture and color.

This class of scope is large with numerous options. It obviously includes 2-8X, 3-9X and 3.5-10X, but I would argue that it also includes 4.5-14X and, perhaps at a maximum, 4-16X and 3-18X scopes. These scopes should have a lower end that is low enough to allow close shooting, but in my thinking, I also put a limit on the upper end—primarily because if you don't need it there is no point in buying it or carrying it.

Higher magnification doesn't make an impossible shot possible, but it makes reasonable shots easier. Go up to 9X and a difficult shot at longer range is simplified because you can see both target and aiming point

Boddington's classes of magnification are represented by (bottom to top) a Weaver 1.25-5X (low range), Nikon 3-9X (medium range) and Bausch & Lomb 6-24X (high range). The low-and high-range scopes have limited utility, and most shooters are well served by the medium-range.

The low-range scopes, typically thought of for dangerous game or close-range shooting, have small objectives—making them poor choices for low-light conditions.

within the target better. Go on up to 12, 14 or even 16 or 18X, and longer targets are even more visible.

There's a limit, though. Mirage is also magnified, often making it difficult to actually use extreme magnification, and in the world of big game hunting, there is really little utility in magnification above 14X or so.

This class of scope has an enlarged objective bell with a larger objective lens. Just how big it should be depends somewhat on the application, but again, all things being equal, a larger objective gathers more light. So by combining a greater range of magnification with enhanced light-gathering capability, this group is far and away the most versatile.

The scopes in what I would call the high-end variable category compose a small group with the most limited utility. For instance, 4-24X scopes have been around for a while, and CounterSniper has a 3-25X scope. But these are large scopes, bulky and usually heavy, and in my view have high-range settings—20X and beyond—that are too powerful to be useful for most field applications.

Mind you, there are purposes for such scopes. They may not do the average deer hunter much good, but they are exactly what the doctor ordered for varmint hunters (woodchucks, prairie dogs and such).

These big scopes are also useful for any and all targets to be addressed at very long ranges. I make no secret that I have a major ethical problem with shooting at big game at extreme distances, but there are no range limits in the tactical world. Also, whether punching paper or ringing steel plates, it's a lot of fun to stretch the envelope.

Construction

As I mentioned, scope power is only one piece of the puzzle. Riflescopes are not created equal, and generally you get what you pay for. On the range and in the field, you can see the benefit of the best glass with the best coatings—especially in low light and at long range. You cannot neces-

sarily see the difference in the store, and certainly not in a catalog, but the optics market is extremely competitive, so you can generally accept that there are good reasons why one riflescope from Brand A costs a lot more than a riflescope of identical size and magnification from Brand B.

In optics quality counts in all ways. Theoretically, a 3-9X scope with a 50mm objective lens (3-9x50) will gather more light than a 3-9X with a 36mm objective lens—but only if quality of lenses, coatings and assembly are equal. Obviously, I prefer a hunting scope that will help me see

better in those critical periods at dawn and dusk, but there are limits. In North America we don't do much night shooting, so we have little genuine need for a classic European riflescope with a huge 56mm objective lens. If you don't need the extra glass, there's little reason to pay for it or to carry it.

My biggest beef with extra-large objective lenses is that they have to be mounted so high. Unlike Europeans, who commonly shoot at night and learn to shoot with the head erect and stock contact at the jawline (to accommodate high scopes), we

Even if the country you hunt is relatively open, most game is going to be active at dawn and dusk, so you want an optic that gathers light without overdoing it. Lighted reticles can be a help, too.

Today's big zoom ranges put a lot of power into the variable, and it's good to be able to dial up and see your target better. Modern reticles with additional aiming points further increase the ability to connect at longer ranges.

usually learn to shoot with the head down and the "spot weld" on the cheek. If you need to raise your head to see through the scope, you may have too much scope on that rifle.

For many years, the American standard tube diameter was one inch, while the European standard was 30mm, and as I mentioned, the 34mm tube is becoming more common. All things being equal (once again), a larger tube gathers more light. Here is where quality starts to make a major difference: A really good one-inch tube scope may be brighter than an inexpensive 30mm scope of similar size and power. And, conversely, a really good 30mm tube "dangerous game" scope with a straight objective may well gather more light than an inexpensive scope with a huge objective lens. Quality comes first, and comparisons are valid only between scopes of similar quality.

There is another benefit to the larger tube diameter, and that is increased windage and elevation adjustment, which comes into play in long-distance shooting. Few things are more frustrating than trying to dial in on a distant target and running out of adjustment.

Reticles

There are a ton of reticles on the market these days, and to my thinking, choosing a reticle is almost always a compromise. The finer the reticle the more precise the aim, but the bolder the reticle the more quickly the eye is drawn to the center. For shooting prairie dogs at long range the finest, thinnest crosshair is just fine, but as the light starts to go you will have increasing difficulty seeing the thin wires. This is why the various plex-type reticles with heavy outer wires surrounding a finer center are so versatile and so popular.

If shooting at longer range is of interest, then I strongly believe in reticles with additional aiming points. In this context, "longer range" means shooting at any distance that requires holdover. Additional aiming points on the vertical crosswire just plain beat the hell out of "Kentucky elevation."

The mil-dot system is pretty universal in the tactical world, but most optics companies have their own more or less proprietary systems. My advice: Find one, preferably not too complex, learn to use it and stick with it.

The other option, of course, is to dial the range using adjustable turrets. For really serious long-range work, dialing is more precise but also slower and, in the hunting arena, more prone to error. Although I've done a lot of dial-up shooting in range settings, I have never touched a turret while hunting. So clearly my comfort zone is a range-compensating reticle.

In recent years I have become a true believer in lighted reticles for most big game hunting. It is amazing how quickly the eye is drawn to the center and how quickly that centered spot of light can be superimposed on the target. This is a "bell and whistle" that if you don't think you need you shouldn't pay for and shouldn't carry, but if you haven't messed around with a lighted reticle don't dismiss it until you have.

So now you know how I approach scope choice. I still think the good old 3-9X (or similar) is awfully hard to beat for sheer versatility. This is the class of scope I use most frequently, with modest objectives from 36mm to 50mm.

That said, it's easy to get spoiled by magnification. I'll never forget making the transition from fixed 4X to the 3-9X variable. Today I'm quite sure that any good 3-9X or 3.5-10X will handle any shot I need to take. Even so, I note that 3-12X and 4.5-14X scopes have somehow found their way onto the rifles I'm most likely to use for mountain hunting.

For my purposes, I don't see ever taking another step up in power, and, of course, for many applications I use much smaller scopes. Interest in both "tactical" and "long range" (neither of which is clearly defined) is changing things, but I don't think the basic rules have changed. You get what you pay for, but it's silly to pay for (and then have to carry) more scope than you really need.

The goal is to mount a scope low enough on the rifle that you get a good cheek weld, which leads to correspondingly better field accuracy.